The Washington Coup

Robert Schramm Burnside

Author of: *Coup d'état* [2003]

JFK and the World Oligarchs [2012]

2020 - The Year of the New World Order [2020]

January, 2021.

Copyright 2020, 2021 by Robert Schramm Burnside.

This work is one of personal analysis and opinion by the author. The author is solely responsible for the contents of this work. No responsibility for the contents of his work is assumed by another party.

A reader may email burnside24u at yahoo dot com with questions or requests.

Table of Contents

Index [use a find]

The Setting

The Washington Coup discusses the theory of Allied social systems, how the oligarchs operate, why the Washington coup occurred, and what actions an individual should consider to succeed in and contribute to society. It's time to dismiss fake news and deal in non-fiction.

Will the weak dollar cause the United States to do a financial *reset*? Will the doomsday-glacier Thwaites melt and flood New York City?

The answers are, "Probably" and "Probably". Our children's children may end up managing an organic farm on the high ground near Austin or mining on a distant planet. They'll need what everyone needs - the big picture, skills and knowledge, diversified assets, family, and friends.

The United States democracy isn't broken. It was built strong, but fragile; honest, but dishonest.

The English, Europeans, and Russians were the grand schemers. Their organizational concepts were described in 1848 by French historian Frederic Bastiat in *The Law*:

> *"Where plunder becomes a way of life for a group of men living together in society, they create for themselves in the course of time, a legal system that authorizes it and a moral code that glorifies it."*

Bastiat wrote "of men". The oligarchs running schemes in 1848 were men. Women had no say. Men ran the government,

religions, the military, and the mafias. Those ruthless men are still around, and a woman needs special qualities to break the barrier. Hillary Clinton came within a hair of qualifying.

The richest men run the world and are called oligarchs. They made fortunes because they were in position at the right time. They made the money, kept it, and bonded with other oligarchs to make more money. Now, they are puppeteers; they bid to control the politicians and they partner with international oligarchs.

The English have been U.S. mentors since WW I. Between 1909-1913, Cecil Rhodes and other John Ruskin disciples, like Lord Alfred Milner, established think-tanks in the chief British dependencies and the United States. In the U.S., the English think-tank was the Council of Foreign Relations [CFR].

Winston Churchill and Franklin Roosevelt had their staffs use the CFR's Grand Area plans to define a world-order structure they put into effect after WW II. Churchill and Roosevelt installed CFR plans to allowed Allied oligarchs to avoid another world war, consolidate power, and share the best of a one-world society. They controlled critical resources and maintained the strongest military on the planet.

The Grand Area plans included a concept where the Allied nations enlarged a conflict with another nation, an adversary the media could demonize. Russia was the first Allied adversary. Communism was depicted as being worse than Nazism. This emphasis helped Jack Kennedy become president when he outmaneuvered Richard Nixon by appearing to be more anti-communist during the first presidential debate on television.

Jack was also helped when his father, Joe Kennedy, flew to Chicago and paid off Sam Giancana's representative for delivering the Illinois vote.

Today's sheep are being taught the Allied nations have a new world order [NWO] where China is the adversary. No! This is a staged lie. China is a partner. There's only room for two major players, and preferably they are on opposite sides of the globe. The oligarchs have their pawns orchestrate new scripts so they can control nations in order to enjoy in the best of life. As on Broadway, many new plays have Jewish directors.

To complicate our scenario, a digital revolution is evolving; software is taking control of cars, weather, companies, and even people. Technology is accelerating and eliminating better-paying jobs. We are at the cusp of a cleansing of capitalism, communism, and democracy.

When robots destroy the jobs, there will be some unhappy people because the projection is that the public will be earning 25% less in real earnings. With the advanced software comes complete control. Governments may put computer monitors on every street corner to eliminate crime. Even oligarchs may be monitored to contain their greed.

Work from home will be more acceptable for technocrats. There's also greater mobility in society. Hundreds of thousands of people are migrating away from areas where the taxes are exorbitant or jobs have disappeared. They're moving to states offering better opportunities. Austin is the new Silicon Valley. Bye, bye to older cities and germ-infested subways.

Our current social evolution took 75 years. At the end of WW II, the Allied nations agreed to use the Pentagon as their military think-tank; NATO and Congress became the theatres for the public production. Congress and the President passed legislation to give the U.S. oligarchs an edge. The political parties built layers of bureaucracy, and the oligarchs took a greater share of wealth.

Some of the public is now asking why a few nations have universal healthcare, free college tuition, paid maternity leave, and more vacation time. Simply put, a few nations created more efficient social structures; their leaders made better decisions; their oligarchs were less greedy, and their military didn't act as the arm of the Allied nations.

A few nations allowed scholars to discuss real issues, but the Allied sheep have not been encouraged to discuss the scheming oligarchs or to question their decisions. As Voltaire noted, "If you want to know who controls you, look at who you are not allowed to criticize [or even discuss]."

George Orwell said liberty meant the right to tell people what they do not want to hear. Orwell said the same about democracy, implying liberty and democracy have commonality. Orwell's book, *1984*, implied liberty and democracy were disappearing.

The most prominent Allied oligarch groups are Jewish, Catholic, and WASP. They have bonded to run the world. They use religion, mafias, the military, legal systems, politics, the media, and international partners as a shield to control their sheep.

The Jewish and Catholic groups are the more dominant. The Jewish oligarchs are the mid-town group and the Catholics are the small-town group. Each group has a mafia and uses government intelligence agencies as legal mafias.

The Anglo-Saxon oligarchs, the WASPs, seem to have lost some power since the end of WW II. The Royal Navy is not quite as royal, but the Queen is still in the game.

The oligarchs' advisors come up with diabolical political scripts. Candidates are generally not good managers. They aren't capable of formulating complex strategies; they don't have the resources to stage major dramas.

Chris Hedges wrote a book titled *America: The Farewell Tour*. One of the book's chapters is on gambling. It analyzes Donald Trump's management of his Atlantic City casinos. Trump's game was to get as much financing as possible, strip out money for himself as the project ran, let the business fall apart, bring in dozens of lawyers to hold off bankruptcy while he continues to extract the revenue, and then let the operation go into bankruptcy.

If you had read Hedges' analysis, you probably would never have voted for Donald Trump. In 2016, many Americans did not get what they thought they voted for when they voted for Trump because as president, Trump was his typical greedy self. He managed his presidency the way he managed his casinos. He raked off money and took the U.S. to the verge of bankruptcy. The oligarchs set the stage to imprison the masses.

During the early phase of Trump's presidency, because of what appeared to be an attempted bribery in the Ukraine, Congress debated impeaching Trump. My prior book, *2020 – The Year of the New World Order*, explained why I thought Robert Mueller was a CIA person appointed to head the FBI. Mueller had deftly handled the Manuel Noriega case. Noriega did not testify about CIA drug smuggling or any involvement with the Bushes. In the end, Noriega conveniently died before he left prison.

Robert Mueller jokingly skated through the impeachment hearings. When a Republican senator went on a long tirade, after minutes of directed diatribe, Mueller calming ask, "Would you repeat the question?" What a great "F%$k off!"

As the impeachment hearings concluded, a perfectly staged pandemic clouded the nation. Millions of workers lost their jobs, businesses closed, and panic ensued as an elusive Covid-19 wave overlapped the contested election.

As the election approached, the GOP's racially-biased groups were supported by a new group called Q or QAnon. QAnon, Proud Boys, Women for America First, Stop the Steal, Oath Keepers, Three Percenters, and other right wing organizations drove the hysteria of Trump's campaign rallies. The rebellious groups were organized by the oligarchs' pawns – the GOP, the CIA, and the media. They caused chaos in California, Washington, and other areas where there was an anti-GOP majority.

The GOPs' Deep State includes sophisticated movie producers, and the public bought in and went down the rabbit hole, caught up in rebellious actions. QAnon claimed Trump was secretly aided by the military, and by all indications, they were right.

In December 2020, some of the Trump supporters began to give up the chase. After the votes were recounted in several states and dozens of fraud suits were thrown out, on December 2, Attorney General William Barr acknowledged there was no widespread fraud.

The rioting continued after the Georgia senate race, when the Democrats won control of the Senate. At that point, the Democrats had no reason to riot. Still, in several cases, the GOP controlled media blamed the riots on the Democrats. This was really an indication of the media's GOP connection.

On January 5, the aftermath of months of confrontation had built up for the last act in Washington, a coup. As Liz Cheney brought forth the knife for Donald Trump's administration, thousands of protestors were set to *storm* the U.S. Capitol. The media, the President, and the GOP influenced the Washington rioters, but it had to be planned at the top by the oligarchs through military intelligence. With their intelligence networks, the military is really the only U.S. group with the sheer power to orchestrate a coup.

What was the larger script? Why did the Deep State go overboard and distort reality? Simple: The oligarchs realized that in the future there would be no need for oligarchs if there was truth. The U.S. won't need lawyers, religious leaders, or a large military. The sheep would need sound goals to accomplish the world's most important objective: to change focus from war to living as a peaceful society.

Although the Grand Area plans are becoming obsolete, the military and the oligarchs want to continue ruling, and now they want to control the galaxy. This view is similar to when the monarchs realized the world was round. After Magellan's voyage, the race was on to colonize land on all the continents.

A theory, "first in last out [FILO]," was hypothesized by Russian physicist Alexander Berezin. Berezin's theory postulates the first conquerors of space will take control of one galaxy after another, and we appear to be the first explorers of space.

Trump's administration set up a space agency to begin to advance space technology using taxpayer money. Contracts were awarded Elon Musk's SpaceX corporation. SpaceX is completing a Beta test of communication satellites orbiting around the earth. This will enable the oligarch's military to have high-speed communications with their troops anywhere on the planet.

Space exploration seems destined to change our lives; whoever wins will control the robots. Will it be the hierarchical oligarchs or scholars or aliens?

There may be repercussions for communication companies as wealth shifts hands. The snake-charmers - Noam Chomsky, Henry Kissinger, Bill Clinton, Joe Biden, Kamala Harris, Jinping Xi, Vladimir Putin, the Queen, and the Pope - will facilitate. If there are anti-gravity space-ships, the oligarchs must control the profits. The sheep will be left to flock about without a piece of the action.

Paradise is not in space. Look at the beautiful streams, mountains, and the elk. Paradise is right here. Why go to another planet? We just need to redefine our society's social structure.

We have lost control of our finances and the population. Oh, we do have a rule of law - oligarch's law!

We haven't seen aliens because they aren't stupid. There is no money to be made zipping around in space. It would cost too much to mine gold. Besides, it would destroy the market, which the oligarchs already control.

In all likelihood, space will offer an alternate planet to escape to after we mess our planet up. We are approaching that situation, and aliens may have an alternate planet already picked out. They may be out there working on it.

For centuries, on all major subjects, the public has been kept uninformed. The oligarchs herded the sheep so the elites could pretend they had special qualities. This left the masses unpredictable. They seldom analyzed situations correctly. They never saw the black swan coming.

Now, our circumstances have suddenly changed. The Middle East belongs to the Allied group. That's why a bolder approach is being taken, especially with Palestinians.

The timing of this transition is tremendously important. Past events pale in comparison to what's occurring. Multiple nations have nuclear resources; some nations are putting weapons in space. The oligarchs need to acknowledge to the masses they have friendly agreements so we can peacefully move forward. The nations' need to meet to reorganize the world's social structures, but it doesn't appear that the oligarchs want an informed public.

Colonel Shanghi Pierce was a Texas cattle rancher with a huge spread. In the 1890s, Pierce fenced in 400 acres of my great grandfathers' land in Wharton county. I almost urinated on Pierce's grave because of that.

In *Cow People*, J. Frank Dobie described Pierce's response when he was asked by a younger church-person, "Mr. Pierce, do you really think there is a heaven?"

"I doubt it son. I don't see how the good Lord would voluntarily take upon himself the immense job of cutting back so many culls in the human race."

Pierce's white Lord wasn't stupid enough to take the time to cull the sheep - just plow them under. Pol Pot, Stalin, Napoleon, LeMay, and perhaps even Churchill would have agreed!

This may be a culling moment. It may be time to take care of the pollution and population problems. Our planet can't continue to fill the ocean floors with plastic and pesticides. What are we, a colony of human roaches?

Our mental state has been severely disrupted by the Washington coup. To use a Chris Hedges' quote, "Spend enough in war or prostitution [or under Trump or in a pandemic] and you will … become numb, dominated by paranoia and deeply distrustful. You lash out, sometimes physically, at whatever or whoever you perceive to be a threat. You become a hunted animal. You divide the world between predators and prey." [Y01]

****

Franklin Roosevelt said, "In politics nothing happens by accident. If it happens, it was planned that way."

This was similar to Joe Kennedy's, "Things don't happen [of themselves]; they are made to happen in the public relations field. [Y02]

The new world order began when Richard Nixon negotiated the US-China deal. China was a more ideal adversary than Russia. They were on the opposite side of the globe, removed from Europe and the United States. China had millions of workers in the rice paddies.

Xi Jinping pretends to be an adversary so his oligarchs can share in the good life. The Allied nations helped modernize China by signing one-sided business agreements, shifting power away from Russia. This pressured Russia, and when Brown & Root built Russia's oil pipeline to Europe, Russia became a U.S. partner. When was the last time a Russian spy was caught? The Russians have our codebook and we have theirs. Vladimir Putin is our friend, and we appropriately give him shade!

The Chinese have the same view of North Korea as the Allied nations - merge North and South Korea. Therefore, China *must* also be one of our future partners. It's a game! If they weren't partners, they wouldn't be our adversary.

Whoever hacked the U.S. could be the adversary of the moment. No one is believable. Mike Pompeo said Russia hacked the U.S. Trump countered by saying it was the Chinese. It might have been the CIA hacking themselves for job security!

The JFK assassination, Nixon's negotiation with China, and the empowerment of Donald Trump were powerful events. Trump was galvanizing. His presidency was a turning point.

Trump was a sadist, bully, authoritarian, and casino owner. Trump didn't have any permanent campaign managers. If you weren't a relative or a sycophant, Trump ran you off — "You're resigned."

Trump's skill set included extensive Chapter 11 experience, knowledge of property development, and the ability to lie. Trump proudly packed the courts with judges who would support a static Constitution.

Trump was protected by Israeli intelligence and lawyers like William Barr, Rudy Giuliani, and Alan Dershowitz. Attorney General William Barr, like George W. Bush, came from a family that had Rockefeller ties. Barr's grandfather was Jewish and he worked with John McCloy to prosecute Germans at the end of WW II. McCloy was David Rockefeller's financial mentor.

Barr may be publicly spoken of harshly, but he was *the* powerhouse of Trump's administration. Barr saved Trump from being thrown out of office; Barr faced down Rupert Murdock when FOX contested Trump; Barr told the world that there was no voter fraud before he exited holding his smiling face down.

Trump's son-in-law, Jared Kushner, has powerful Israeli connections, and Trump did everything possible to patronize Israel. Trump's support also included the CIA, mafias, British allies, and our Russian partner, Vladimir Putin.

As part of Trump's mafia collusion, Trump went out of his way not to release JFK assassination evidence. Trump implied he would release JFK evidence, as had been mandated decades earlier, but his executive order closed that door. Barr assisted when Barr's people in the DOJ defined online gambling as illegal. This rewarded casino owners.

Donald Trump did some things that were important and necessary. He wasn't always right, and he was frequently bold. Because of his nature and attitudes, many regarded him as less than presidential; they thought he belonged either in jail or in an insane asylum. Trump's biggest failure was that he wanted to be a scientist and a manager. Science, corporate management, and software were outside of Trump's nature and his intellectual domain.

Trump's largest monetary contributions came from casino owners like the Adelsons and the Fertittas - Tilman, Frank, and Lorenzo. This should have been highlighted by the media, but the media seldom if ever delivers substance.

The Deep State colludes with the media to dumb down the sheep to extend the oligarch's game. The public could be enlightened. Like China, the U.S. oligarchs could be more selective of candidates for decision-making roles. The oligarchs could choose an intelligent authoritarian as a presidential candidate.

Nations no longer need the Deep State and middlemen. The question is, "Will the oligarchs voluntarily loosen the masses' chains?"

Absolutely, "No"! The thought of a tuned-in public is why elites use candidates like Trump and Biden. The elites are afraid the masses will realize how they've been duped. Why else would the U.S. have dysfunctional candidates?

In 2020, Donald Trump ran against an old, memory-impaired politician, Joe Biden. Mark Cuban, Bernie Sanders, and Elizabeth Warren were more qualified, but toxic behavior was acceptable because chaos is the prod for herding sheep.

The oligarchs couldn't risk nominating someone with answers; they felt safe with Trump because there was so much damaging evidence on Trump. The oligarchs thought they could contain Trump, but Trump was like Saudi oil - limitless.

Biden would have won if he were dead. That's why the voting lines were half a mile long in places. "You won't give us a mere $1,200, while you give the elites trillions?"

At the RNC, Trump Junior realized the 3AM tweets weren't working when he lamented, "It will not turn out well for Donald."

Trump earmarked himself to be the villain; his personality was too strong.

The oligarchs orchestrate the Deep State of both parties. The pawns are stary-eyed, and they can be bought. If not, they'll be abruptly squeezed out!

The border wall, China as an adversarial, UFO information, the California fires, QAnon, and the potential for a financial "reset" were part of a two-party scripted play.

A $100B border wall and people being bused to the border was presented in order to focus Americans away from the trillions of dollars that were being stolen.

The sheep weren't allowed to see what was going on! The public witnessed riots and fires. Facebook became a battleground. The media and the intelligence agencies, and their sycophants, the mafias, encouraged the red-necked sheep to believe there would be a draining of the swamp - that never-Trumpers would be challenged by the AG or the legal system.

The oligarchs used the executive powers to excite the fascism woven into the United States' fabric. They knew the public's characteristics were:

1) Risk Avoidance: A person is trained to avoid conflicts. Ask anyone to help enlighten the public, and he will shy away if he's not young and stupid. After decades of wars and controversy, a senior will avoid risk, especially if all he has to do is to look the other way. This is political correctness.

2) Sedimentary Memory: In the 1800s, a settlers' average life expectancy may have been 50 years. Today, it's closer to 75. Older people develop fixed opinions, automatically rejecting information. The sedimentary types don't store new facts in their memories, and that may be why criminologists have found people over age 40 pose little risk to society regardless of their pasts. [Y03]

3) Media Facilitation: The media speaks to those in sedimentary decline and the closed-minded public. They know the sheep avoid risk and that the elderly will never understand the virtual world. The facilitators avoid discussing elites and real issues. They carefully elevate associates who add to their inconsequential dialog.

Forget terms like middle- or lower-class. We have a two-class system evolving. All of Congress is bought and paid for! Talk of elites, facilitators, and sheep.

Analyze your surroundings by making unbiased political statements. When others present their views as fact, determine those who are open-minded. Pan out sedimentary and closed-minded associates.

The Rothschilds turned Communism and Socialism into a democracy with a two-party system controlled by the same group. The English oligarchs perfected the game of controlling the two-party system and allowing conservatives to squabble with the liberals. Now they televise it!

People have conservative and liberal views. Opinions are formulated by experiences. As an example, white people from Biloxi, Mississippi are more racist because Jefferson Davis's home is nearby. Some have never acknowledged losing the Civil War.

The elite groups are bonded. They're funded with taxpayer money.

Terms like progressive, populist, autocrat, neocon, technocrat, authoritarian, BLM, and QAnon are used to segment the sheep.

Socrates said, "When the debate is lost, slander becomes the tool of the loser." Today, there's no debate of issues before the slander begins. The masses can't move past racism and mismanagement to discuss the failed social structure. The voters are easily caught up in media noise; no one can rise through disinformation.

Most of the public believes the oligarchs are sincere, even though former DCIA Mike Pompeo explained how the CIA operates: "We lied; we cheated; we stole."

The public failed to hear Frederick Douglass: "Power concedes nothing without a demand; it never has and it never will."

"We have to start with the truth." Julian Assange

An open and realistic dialog is the way an individual can escape, but the public is afraid to talk about reorganizing society. People saw how Julian Assange was persecuted. They won't risk being accused of anarchy or anti-Semitism.

There are several reasons the oligarchs created this chaos. First, when Allied troops got rid of ISIS, the game was over, except for a few dummies trying to hang on. This immediately changed how things are done. Our new Allied control allowed the Israelis to pound the Palestinians.

Under Trump, the Catholics and the Israelis repaired their split caused by the JFK assassination. That wasn't Trump's plan. The oligarchs make the plans. The oligarch clans control the U.S. power, and with the DOJ reporting to the President, there is no higher-law to protect the public.

Justice is just one part of the problems. Over two decades ago, Ross Perot warned the public when he wrote in *United We Stand*, "We can't keep living beyond our means. We can't survive an irresponsible government."

The United States has not survived the last irresponsible administrations, and the public sheep shouldn't wait to see the black swan. Here is the unseen: Everything is a game – football, politics, religion, and all of civilization, including the quest for world power.

Each year, the game changes and gets slightly more complex. The puppeteers funding the game understand the complexities. The only thing left for oligarchs and intellectuals to discuss is cheating! Cheating is always behind a façade of honor and duty. Winners almost always cheat in a grand fashion. Napoleon Bonaparte understood: "The surest way to remain poor is to be an honest man."

To understand any game, one must appraise the weak points in order to write patents and laws. That's why we have a rule of [oligarchs'] law – so SCOTUS can keep our nation's

Constitution and laws rigid because that's what allows the oligarchs to maintain control.

The Astros took baseball cheating one trashcan too far, but what a great team!

Trump expanded the political rules, and he put voters on the cusp of a coup. The extent of Trump's last-ditch efforts to stay in office frightened Europeans.

The game will change drastically within a few years because software will manage everything. This should be a boon for mankind; instead, the term "reset" is being murmured by insiders and the smart money is exiting the U.S. The elites' rigged system has bankrupted the middle-class.

When Ronald Reagan lowered the oligarchs' taxes from over 70% to less than 30%, the middle-class was set up to be destroyed. Women entered the work force as real wages went down, and the elites kept more of the profits. In 50 years, there was no trickle-down. And, Bill Clinton did not help by reducing capital gains.

Sheep were told the U.S. could remedy their situation by extracting tariffs from China. That didn't work. Now the gurus are testing a digital currency. In 2020, seven banks, including the Bank of England [BOE], began their Beta tests. After this test, experts expect the value of the U.S. dollar to weaken. The digital currency system will allow the oligarchs more control. This doesn't help the public.

The masses need leadership. Quoting Tilman Fertitta, "Leadership isn't something you impose on other people. The fact of the matter is people want to be led – and more specifically, they want to be led by great leaders. [Y04]

Rule 1: Become a leader; develop technical skills and work your way from the bottom up. Associate with the right people and care about others. Pitch in; carry out the garbage. When necessary, bend the rules, hit the trashcan, and succeed!

Competence and Religion

Russ Ross proved a success in three fields – energy, medical, and gaming. Russ spent nineteen years with M.D. Anderson. He saved Anderson millions of dollars.

Russ told me about a technical person at Anderson who wasn't quite as brilliant, but he had managed to stay long enough to advance to his level of incompetence. Eventually, upper management recognized Mr. X's usefulness had expired, so during a period of mismanagement, Anderson let him go.

Mr. X's wife had a high position with a competitive hospital, and she was able to influence the competitor to offer Mr. X a management job.

One day, Mr. X called Russ to ask a technical question. His group was using UNIX and he thought the system should be migrated to another platform. Russ told Mr. X that UNIX was a perfect platform for what his group was supporting.

Russ advised Mr. X not to try to be creative. Russ told Mr. X to seek the advice of his staff because the function of managers at his level was not to be the technical experts. Mr. X's function should be to listen to his experienced staff.

Of course, Mr. X didn't take Russ's advice. He attempted to become a creative, problem-solver, but he was so bad that his staff stopped showing up when he called technical meetings. Eventually, Mr. X's incompetence became apparent to upper management. They decided they had to fire someone, but they couldn't discern who was competent on Mr. X's staff. So, they replaced the entire staff.

Russ concluded by saying, "In larger organizations, managers need to be managers, not primary problem solvers."

Like Mr. X, a few centuries ago religious management was inept. That caused Voltaire to say, "For seventeen hundred years the Christian sect has done nothing but harm."

Christian religions now have professional management. Catholics and Protestants have given up pretending to be warriors or scientists. They no longer tell the sheep that the sun revolves around the earth. Religious professionals need to keep their mouths shut. When one's product is air, he or she has to avoid creativity.

That's also what Trump didn't understand.

The adversarial game exists in many forms, and terminology is a weapon used against adversaries. If you were a conservative, you took sides against "liberals" and "socialists". Republicans used those terms to smear Democrats.

Christians took a stance against "atheists" and "agnostics", and they were willing to go to war to defend their moral code.

Times change! Christianity has become more politically correct. Some religions now embrace non-believers. That may be because military intelligence has become so adept at monitoring people that the government has encroached on the Christian's domain. Communion isn't quite as secretive as it once was.

Religion provides an escape to a moral and honorable world. Religion is extremely significant in the United States. Religion gives families a vision of rewards they'll receive for hard work and obeying moral standards. To be granted the rewards, the farmers and ranchers believe they must struggle to survive. If you draw a line from Austin, Texas to Ft. Wayne, Indiana, those Catholic and Protestant farmers along the roads believe in the hereafter.

On the other side of the believers are those who believe life has a scientific basis - mostly math and digital. They believe religion has no technical basis.

Richard Dawkins, in *The God Delusion*, does a thorough job of examining religion. Dawkins offers this poignant George Carlin quote:

"Religion has actually convinced people that there's an invisible man - living in the sky - who watches everything you do, every minute of every day. And the invisible man has a special list of ten things he does not want you to do. And if you do any of these ten things, he has a special place, full of fire and smoke and burning and torture and anguish, where he will send you to live and suffer and burn and choke and scream and cry forever and ever 'til the end of time . . . But He loves you!"

If the United States got into a debate on reorganizing the U.S. Constitution, the masses would make the subject of religion prominent. The oligarchs would chime in and agree because they use religion as a weapon to control the sheep. The military would also offer support because religion gives a nation a built-in spy organization.

Napoleon Bonaparte understood religion when he said, "Religion is what keeps the poor from murdering the rich."

When Napoleon had to restore the military back to a productive, domestic group, to get soldiers to go back to work, Napoleon reintroduced religion so the soldiers would work in anticipation of the rewards in the hereafter.

When the Declaration of Independence was signed, religion was *supposedly* held apart from politics, but Christian religions and the GOP form of conservatism go hand in hand.

Religion always seeks more power. Religious groups collude and form alliances with political parties to participate in governing. The larger the religious group, the more power it seeks.

Since Lyndon Johnson's administration, racism has caused the white race to flee the Democratic Party. The GOP has gone out of its way to destroy integration. The GOP made politics a war of winners versus losers, where the winners are white, religious people.

Russell Kirk's authoritative book, *The Conservative Mind*, defined the first canon of conservatism as the belief that divine intent ruled society, and logic was secondary. Kirk's third canon espoused a class system, which was a cornerstone of English conservatism.

Kirk's book won high praise from stalwart conservatives like Richard Nixon and William Buckley Jr., and since the 1950s, the GOP has been on a conservative agenda sponsored by white-racist oligarchs.

In the last half-century, the Texas Republicans brought Evangelicals into their fold. The Texas GOP embraced evangelicals and evangelists - people like John Hagee, Pat Robertson, and Billy Graham.

The Moral Majority joined the GOP cause. The Christian leaders spread a 2,000-year-old story of legacy. They claimed Israel should own all the land to the sea. Why? Just a lie!

Religion is about power and money. The Jewish clan and the Catholics run the U.S. because those groups control the two main societies and they use their rule of law. The Jewish Syndicate controls mid-town and the Catholics control small-town. Each has a major mafia and they work together.

The Jewish Syndicate and the Catholics have again joined to control the world. The JFK assassination is old news. Isn't that interesting?

The English WASPs have their mafia - British intelligence. They made Julian Assange an example.

Power shifted as religious actors matured. They understand what land, deeds, money, and power mean.

If you're an Evangelical you have the ultimate chip. You can be "born again." A rancher I knew from near Comanche, Texas had an affair with his high school sweetheart. Jimmy made a mistake and he left the Hico motel receipt in his billfold. By nature, Jimmy's wife got curious about the edge of that receipt sticking out of his billfold. The next thing

Jimmy knows, she has packed up, gone to a motel, and called her lawyer.

Jimmy can visualize the big ranch being divided, but then he hears the word, "Go see her. Talk to her! Tell her you have heard my word. Tell Marge how much you love her, and that this has all been an unfortunate misunderstanding."

Marge, being a good Baptist, listens and buys in, but she asks the preacher to join them so Jimmy can share. The preacher is savvy. He asks Jimmy, "You don't mind sharing this with the congregation, do you?"

Jimmy can't refuse. God's *word* is his trump card.

Religions will have significance as long as the mafias are powerful. Religions have to have a mafia for protection, and the military is supported by religions and the mafias.

There are two major U.S. mafias, if the CIA isn't counted. Joseph Valachi, the original Mafia informant for the *Valachi Papers*, said, "You know, if it wasn't for the Jews, there wouldn't be any organized crime because the Jews finance organized crime. The Italians [Catholics] do what the Jews tell them."

There is no God who speaks to some people some of the time. Master documents like the Bible are a hodge-podge. Concepts like 72 virgins, magic pants, gold tablets, and a holy spirit are not as believable as they once were.

The Russians and Chinese leaders know that if there were "a" God, there wouldn't be dozens of religions and dozens of Gods.

Religious groups use this big lie. They believe they should run the world. The big lie gave the GOP control, and allowed President Reagan to unjustly tax the non-whites. Now the GOP's reign is coming to an end because of the increased percentage of non-whites in the population.

Religion has to be kept in place. The Allied world can't allow a religion to openly run a large nation. It's okay if a smaller nation is a partner and brings something to the table like a large oil reserve, like the Saudis have.

The game is over for the Muslims in Iran; they won't be a significant player because they aren't sophisticated enough to share control. They can't be trusted. Iran will see the black swan during the Biden administration. That's why China is squeezing down their religious groups and creating a Catholic connection. It's time to squeeze down the number of players.

Rule 2: Compartmentalize religion and don't allow it to control the government. Avoid highlighting religion's big lie. Be careful! Voicing negative opinions about God is a sure way to lose friends and associates.

Fritz and Big Jim

LaGrange, Texas is the county seat in Fayette County and Fayette County was part of the old Austin Colony.

It all seemed so simple in the old days. Dad was a signal-maintainer for the Katy Railroad, the Missouri, Kansas, and Texas Railroad. He had some smart genes. Two of his brothers graduated from med-school with honors during the Depression.

Our home place of about 100 acres was about a mile and a half west of Fayetteville, Texas at Highway 159 and Burnside Road. We had another place of about 50 acres that was wooded with post oaks and yaupon. That was as dad had acquired the land. In the old days, settlers had to have some tillable land, some pasture for animals, and some woods for firewood.

When the Great Depression hit, dad offered $9 an acre for 300 acres of river bottom-land. He lost the bid to someone who bid $12.50 an acre. The place had lots of pecan trees along the Colorado River and the next year the pecan crop was so great it earned enough to pay for the place.

Decades later, dad showed me the place after two oil wells had just been completed on the property.

Dad acquired his second place for $15 an acre. In the 1940s, it was reasonable to pay $20 an acre in Fayette County because you could probably get an oil lease for a dollar an acre per year and make a five percent return. That would beat the banks' four percent interest rate.

Our herd of registered Hereford cattle grew to around 50 head. We also had a couple of Jersey cows for milking. We would steer a Jersey-Hereford calf and fatten it for meat. The deep freeze was always well-stocked. We would trade for pork with our neighbor Elo Hattermann. An occasional deer gave us venison chili.

Years after dad missed buying the river bottom place, dad bought a small deer-hunting place for $100 an acre and within a month he signed an oil lease for $110 an acre, essentially getting that place for free plus $10 an acre. Naturally, his gifted money went to acquire an additional hunting place.

There is luck in life's game, but it only pays to look back if you can learn from it.

As children, we would help wean calves, mend barbed-wire fences, collect eggs in chicken nests, milk a cow before school, pick cotton in the summer heat to earn a few dollars, and swim nude in every clear pool we discovered.

Chores were a minor distraction from adventures with a fishing pole and a great dog named Jack. Living in the country and having the opportunity to hunt, fish, play sports, and eat tremendous home-cooked food [now call organic] was indescribably comfortable.

Decades ago, my son Michael spent a week visiting my parents. He caught bass in the ponds, ate my mother's great home cooking, and went around with dad in his old pickup. After my parents spoiled Michael, he returned with a smile and a question. "Was it always like that?" I nodded and Michael concluded, "Boy, you really had it made."

We did! Everyone had it made. People had time to sit on the porch and talk. It was peaceful and enjoyable. The music and food were so great.

Everything in the country was such a marvelous illusion. There was no television or Internet to bring in the bad – just ourselves and the elements. We might hear whispers, but the adults avoided sharing tragedy with us. We were in an open environment where we could freely roam, void of cars. At each farmhouse, we found a lady with a large glass jar full of big sugar cookies. With them, she offered a glass of milk.

We would catch a grasshopper, barb him on a small hook, and watch the little red cork float about. When it disappeared beneath the surface, a big yellow perch would be at the other end of the line.

How far the red cork went down determined the depth of the school. If the cork went way down, it meant the bait was over a deep hole and the fish were in the depths below the bait. If the cork fell on its side, the school was swimming above the bait.

I didn't realize the significance of a strike. If the cork went way-down, I hammered what I thought was big momma. If the cork just went down a couple of inches, I would wait thinking it was a small bream nibbling on a leg. Seven-year-olds seldom receive professional training at catching big bream.

For our young minds, there wasn't enough time between waking up and going to sleep. There were no televisions, no cell phones, and no Internet. How did a person have all that fun back then without those toys?

No one went hungry or was in a hurry. The rural people were in perfect order. They had very few schedules and conflicts. The locals were German-Czech-Bohemian farmers – mostly Catholic or Lutheran.

I know small-town Catholics. My mother was Catholic, but there was a Star of David in her family crest.

There were no Jews or Italians in Fayetteville. I didn't know they were different until I went to college. There was one Baptist family in Fayetteville and they went to church in Lagrange. Schools were segregated and the African American population was small; most had moved to the bigger cities which offered work.

Wives took care of the housework. Saturday was for the mothers shopping and men catching up on work around the home.

On a cooling Saturday evening, a big moon nestled above the town clock as the children and women were watching the $.12 children's or the $.25 adult's movie. John Wayne or Roy Rogers could be on the big screen.

The men would be nursing a cold Lone Star or Falstaff at Joe's Pastime Club. The town intellectuals played dominos - using chalk on the slate tabletops to keep score. Occasionally billiards was in progress on one of the two tables.

Depending on the season, the domino parlor conversations had an air of excitement as small farmers and ranchers revisited their week. They discussed whether it had rained or was going to. Cotton was the cash crop, and if cotton was being bailed, everyone was interested in prices and the crop.

If the election was coming, then politics came up. If deer season had opened, the question was who had gotten their buck. If the boys or girls had a decent basketball or baseball team, that was the hot subject. If the famous wildcatter Glynn McCarty had a crew drilling an oil well down to the Wilcox, burning the bits off around New Ulm, oil leases were the talking points for the men and it was all about black gold.

Sunday was church and getting together with friends and relatives for a big lunch. Naps, coffee, desserts, and conversation followed. The Pitch card game was popular.

In Texas, on one side you had guys who could shoot, and on the other side guys who could enforce the law - men who knew how to shoot men. The man that kept the peace in Fayette County was Sheriff T.J. "Big Jim" Flournoy. He resided in LaGrange.

One fall, dad invited Big Jim to go white wing hunting at one of our stock ponds. Jim brought his deputy Charlie Prilop with him. Big Jim was 6'4" and Charlie stood around the same height. Big Jim had huge hands and he looked a lot like Lyndon Johnson. Together, Big Jim and Charlie with their big ten-gauge shotguns looked like a couple of guys you would want to avoid.

The pond stood on the side of a hill up from the house, so we had a front-row seat for the action. It was quiet for a while, but at dusk, the doves came like swarms of bees. Jim and Charlie began popping caps like firecrackers. The doves came from all sides - bam, bam, bam.

For all the shooting, the big guys lost the battle. Their eyesight was not that good. They were getting older, but the main reason was the nettle grass. The tank was surrounded by fine purple, 8-inch grass. If you shot a dove and it fell in the nettle grass, and you didn't watch exactly where it landed, you couldn't find it, especially when it got darker.

When Big Jim and Charlie finished busting caps, they came down by the house, and my brother Paul and I talked to them. The discussion centered on Big Jim's pistol. The pistol only had one notch. We got to hold it. It was felt kind of small. Charlie enlarged the pistol when he told us how Jim had drawn it and shot a guy right between the eyes.

Jim acknowledged, "Well, you know when a guy is coming at you with a shotgun, your adrenalin gets to pumping." Then, Jim passed the conversation back to Charlie, "Charlie has the N#$%r killer."

Charlie handed over his big double-barreled ten-gauge. Charlie had been covering the back of a building where a robbery was taking place and he shot a robber when he came out the back.

The big ten-gauge is a Texas lawman's favorite. It sounds like a cannon firing and kicks like a mule. The trick is to hold the butt of the shotgun in the grove of your shoulder when you pull the trigger so your body absorbs the kick. Supposedly Robert Kennedy got knocked to the ground by the kick of a ten-gauge when he was deer hunting at Lyndon Johnson's ranch.

A Dallas ATF agent told me he and his fellow agent once suspected a funeral home hearse was transporting booze in a space below the coffin. One evening they stopped the hearse and asked the driver and his companion to move the coffin so they could see if there was booze in the lower compartment. The driver and his companion hesitated, commenting it would not be right to disturb the dead.

On the distinct clicks of two big ten-gauge triggers, as they were pulled into firing position, the doors of the hearse flew open like a ripe sardine can.

The booze was in the compartment below the coffin. After the agents and had the driver drop off the corpse, they confiscated the hearse. Mission accomplished! It was so exciting, but the next day their leader read them the riot act. "Never, never stop a hearse. What if you didn't find any booze?"

Big Jim and LaGrange achieved fame, of sorts. In the 18th, 19th, and early 20th centuries, there were whorehouses in towns throughout the nation. Women were second class citizens and could not get good-paying jobs. Technical and management jobs were off-limits to women.

Near LaGrange, there was a whorehouse referred to as the Chicken Ranch. The locals called the house of prostitution Old Lady Jesse's after the proprietor. Jesse's was about a mile out of LaGrange off of Highway 71.

ZZ Top even wrote a song about LaGrange because the brothel became famous as the Best Little Whorehouse in Texas.

In an antique book store in Portland, Maine, I found a book on the Best Little Whorehouse. Even though most names were changed, I recognized a few of the locals like Big Jim. The book said Jesse had a typed set of rules for her girls, three full pages. I could almost see Jesse hunting and pecking on the typewriter.

No one around Fayette County talked about Jesse's in social conversation. They didn't have to; everyone knew of the place and Jessie's reputation. When LaGrange went for donations to the new hospital, Jessie immediately responded with a $10,000 donation. Today, that would have been ten times as large. Jessie was always very generous.

The church leaders and town fathers realized that young men needed sexual experience. They didn't want the boys deflowering the local young ladies. The Victorian age meant virginity until marriage, and this was a strict Catholic-Lutheran community. And, there were not many high paying jobs for good-looking women.

Gas was cheap and the Chicken Ranch was close enough to Austin and College Station to entice college boys from The University of Texas and Texas A&M.

Many of the prostitutes were gorgeous. One beautiful brunette named Diane would have made Liz Taylor look like a little girl. Diane was about 5'8" – beautiful and perfectly proportioned.

Diane drove a black Lincoln and was rumored to have a sugar-daddy. For a young man with fire in his veins, it was a quick $5 contribution – perhaps an oil change for her Lincoln.

Francis was another beauty, albeit brown-haired. I had an Aggie friend who hitchhiked in from College Station to LaGrange coming home for the weekend. He got dropped at the gasoline station at the corner of Highway 71 and 77 in LaGrange. After he called his mother to pick him up, he noticed Francis was filling up her car with gasoline. Later that night, after a local dance, he stopped by the Chicken Ranch to see Francis. When he commented on seeing her at the gas station, she replied, "You should have asked. I would have given you a ride home."

[His mother might have asked, "Who was that girl that gave you a lift? Is she from around here?"

"No Mom, just some friend I met at the Chicken Ranch!"]

The ladies were regular people. They were trapped. At the time, there were no great jobs for gorgeous women. Where could they get a job where they would be able to afford a big Lincoln? The famous stripper, Sally Rand, was their leader.

The beautiful female problem always exists. In the 1990s, when I was doing development with Sytek in Silicon Valley, I advertised for a person with heavy communications development experience using assembly language. We were in a transition phase moving to C language.

One person applied. It was a lady who had five years of heavy experience. She was managing two men who had their masters in electrical engineering. She had two drawbacks. She only had about 90 hours of college and she was too good looking.

During the interview, I asked her what she didn't like. She said, "Masters, double E, Taiwanese." That sold me. I had a Taiwanese lady working for me. She was an excellent worker, but strictly 8 to 5 and always wanting the maximum raise. Too picky and not 100% committed!

I asked my manager to interview my potential hire. I told him, "I have a problem," but I didn't tell him what it was.

My boss was the typical masters, double E, Stanford, who drove a Porsche. He interviewed her for almost 30 minutes. When he can out, he said, "She's perfect, but I see your problem. Send her to Human Resources. If she comes back, you have a new hire."

That was the last I saw of her. The nearness of a beautiful woman wearing a hint of fine perfume causes the minds of male software-nerds to turn to putty.

An investigative TV reporter named Marvin Zindler broke the story of the Chicken Ranch as if he had suddenly discovered the place. Marvin's stature had been dwindling and he was trying to reinvent himself. Marvin's new fame was quickly established when he and Big Jim had a confrontation and Marvin got pushed around. Suddenly the Best Little Whorehouse in Texas became the center of attention in every television newscast.

Zindler should have gotten a headstone. Big Jim told my dad two groups offered to kill Zindler, free of charge. The tough element of society would kill someone for you if they respected you.

Jim said he was getting too old, about to retire, so he declined the offers. Jim could have acquiesced because of fierce publicity. Someone wrote a screenplay and a movie with

Burt Reynolds as Big Jim followed. The intense publicity forced the whorehouse to close its doors.

Years later, while doing a landman project for EOG Resources on the old Enron leases, I met an oilman who completed an oil well on the Chicken Ranch property before the whorehouse building was shipped to Dallas and converted into a club. This oilman was from Midland and knew the Bushes. He sold the well to the Clayton Williams Company.

The outspoken Clayton Williams put his foot in his mouth when he ran for governor against Ann Richards. William's lost the race for governor and a joke floated that Saddam Hussein looked in the mirror and asked, "Is there anyone in the world who can put his foot in his mouth more than me?" The mirror responded, "Clayton Williams."

Fritz and his family had a house about a mile on the east side of Fayetteville off highway 159. He was a typical 5'10" German. He ran a dairy and worked as a weigh-master at auction barns.

During WW II, Fritz was the only person around Fayetteville who owned several cattle trailers. On the side, he bought and sold cattle. He could look at a cow or steer and tell you its exact weight.

Before dad got his first truck with a sufficient bed to carry a cow and calf, he would get Fritz to haul a cow or heifer to the auction. One day dad and Fritz took one of dad's cows to the auction in Texas City. They took highway 90 into Houston and then the Gulf Freeway to Texas City.

When they got to the auction barn, a monster Brahma bull jumped off the truck in front of them before he could be weighed. Fritz called to the weigh master above the scales, "Bet you a T-bone dinner I can get closer to his weight."

The response was, "Write it down."

When they compared the weight estimates, they were within 4 pounds. Both estimates were over 1,700 pounds. The bull's weight fell between the estimates and Fritz won the T-bone.

When dad was in his 80s, he told me there had been some cattle rustling around Fayetteville. Cattle were disappearing one or two at a time. It was like someone backed up a cattle trailer, opened the trailer gate, and then used some range cubes or grain to lure a cow in before they closed the gate and drove away.

Dad said, "One day Big Jim showed up in Fayetteville. He talked to a lot of people about the rustling. It kept coming back to Jim that Fritz was the biggest cattle trader - the wheeler-dealer in the area. Jim didn't have any evidence, but he finally talked with Fritz."

Dad smiled as he said, "Jim said he told Fritz that he knew Fritz was involved and if another cow disappeared, he was going to pick Fritz up."

Fritz denied participating, but strangely the rustling ceased.

Dad's story left me with greater respect for Fritz and Big Jim. They were the remnants of the men who remained after the waves of settlers. They were tough, smart, and survivors who achieved a unique position in the community.

Inside the Texas Chicken Ranch by Jayme Lynn Blaschke and published in 2016 by History Press is *the* definitive account of the Best Little Whorehouse and Big Jim.

Those times seem so distant. The people who lived in Fayetteville and LaGrange had a subsistence existence. That was by choice. The Great Depression of the 1930s and WW II made them wary. They didn't squander anything. They expected Big Jim to represent them. They didn't want outsiders taking advantage of them. They loved the land and being almost free.

Texas was unique back then. When Tom Hollingsworth was in college in Austin, he bought a new white Dodge with a long whip aerial. One day he needed to get to his hometown of Dallas as quickly as possible. He put the pedal to the metal and drove as fast as he could up Highway 35. Past Waco the highway patrol stopped him. The patrolman looked him over, checked his id, and told Tom to have a safe trip. He didn't give him a ticket.

Tom's father owned two western-wear stores. Tom was attired a white shirt, black string bowtie, boots, and a fine western hat and coat. I concluded the patrolman mistook Tom for a Texas Ranger.

Years later, I was in Dallas having a late-night breakfast at a restaurant and I saw a man decked out like Tom about to pay his tab and leave. I couldn't help but ask him if he was a Texas Ranger. He responded, "No, but in two weeks I am going to a Ranger Hall of Fame ceremony in Waco."

He was some sort of state officer, so I asked him if he knew Big Jim. Since he did, I said, "Tell me a Big Jim story."

The State had sent him down to check out the Chicken Ranch story. Jim saw him and asked him what he was doing there. After he acknowledged he was there to check out the situation, Jim told him, "If I see you here after dark, I'm going to kill you."

I asked, "Well, what happened after dark."

"I don't know. I didn't hang around."

That confirmed his story was true. Jim had position and his own rules for the game. Think about that! That's what a person needs to control his life.

The 1950s and 1960s were the times of John Wayne, Howard Hughes, Jack Kennedy, and Lyndon Johnson. I got John Wayne's autograph at the Nighthawk in Austin on 19th Street when Wayne came to Austin for the premiere of *The Alamo*.

I've played on the golf course where Hughes played. On one of the tees, my playing partner explained how he played behind Hughes' foursome. Then he teed off with the same wooden club he had used in 1948.

Hughes funded a software company in Houston named Hughes Dynamics. They started with an IBM 7090. Carl Gann, who later managed Anderson Clayton's computer center in Dallas, said that after a year Howard came for a meeting in a tee shirt and tennis shoes with two of his executives. The top executive started the meeting, saying, "You've done an outstanding job, but we have decided to shut this operation down. You have one month to let the clients know and close the doors."

I never met Jack or Jackie Kennedy, but I knew people who did. One met Kennedy at Johnson's ranch.

Capitalism is brutal. It caused Fayetteville to gentrify and transition. Decades ago, the railroad eliminated the passenger service and the cotton gins closed. As the population fell, the freeways improved and it became easier to work from the country and commute to Houston or Austin.

Now, the kids and town people have gotten involved in the Internet. Antiques and restaurants have become more prominent.

Recently, Covid-19 caused an evolution where the rural counties surrounding the large cities prospered as they built a new social order. The pandemic and Zoom will have a lasting effect. People don't need to leave the country to get a higher education to pursue jobs. The Tesla plant near Austin is just over an hour's drive from Fayetteville, and Austin is rapidly becoming the new Silicon Valley.

The rural population has begun to realize the big-city elites consider them to be sheep. Some sheep see that most of the elites won't be needed. The Deep State is expensive overhead, and sheep are starting to understand they will be taken advantage of by the city crowd if they are not careful. Some locals actually want to tax the rich!

Rule 3: As time evolves, social structures mature and technology allows the masses to change their perception of life. A person needs to be aware of what is changing and try to plan ahead of the curve.

Position, Position, Position

"Poker's the only game fit for a grown man. Then your hand is against every man's, and every man's is against yours. Teamwork? Who ever made a fortune by teamwork? There's only one way to make a fortune, and that's to down the fellow who's up against you."

W. Somerset Maugham

Poker is like capitalism. Although poker is a game, playing winning poker has similarities with living a successful life. There is no room for superstition. Life is a numbers game, but every once in a while, a little luck comes into play.

Reading books and collaboration are the best remedies for poor playing of any game. In the same amount of time you can play a session of poker, one can discuss ten hands, or read a couple of chapters.

If you have collaborative friends, then you don't have to play to improve your game. You can read, think, and communicate with collaborators and your game will improve because you vicariously experience their wins and losses.

My main Texas Hold'em collaborator was John Sandberg. No one enjoyed poker as much as John. John came from a family of great poker players, guys who played big in towns like Chicago with people like Jackie Gleason. Their advice to John was, "You need a hand, and then you need to get as much money as you can into the pot, and then you need to win the pot. That sounds simple. Get a hand. Get the money in the pot, and then win.

John learned early to be graceful in winning and losing. There's no reason to try to hurt another player's feelings. John will be the first to tell the loser he got lucky when he busted that person's aces and took the pot with two pairs.

John tells a story about playing in a game for six hours. Another player had come to the table and played for the last hour and a half. He finally looked at John and said, "You haven't played a hand since I sat down."

"Yes, and you've played every hand."

"My wife died two years ago. We had no children. I have no heirs. I like to play."

Enjoyment in the form of action was this player's criteria and he could afford it. John's opponent was the type of player we all look for. The biggest problem in poker and business today is the lack of players willing to gamble or spend money. The days of the sub-prime loan salesman dropping a few thousand in the game are gone.

More players have learned that if they win a big pot, then they become the target of the other players. Unless you're a great player who wants to bait the competition, it's wise science to pick up your winnings from a monster pot and exit as soon as possible. The same lesson applies to life. Our economy is controlled and the life game has become more difficult.

I read a book analyzing all the various styles of play. The author explained how to defeat different strategies. He concluded there was one style of play that couldn't be beaten. No strategy could exploit a conservative playing style.

John's greatest strengths are playing conservative and his understanding of player personalities. His style is simple. He's opposed to taking undue risk. He looks for a balance where he has consistency in his results.

You must learn to play the game where you win at least half of the time, most ideally enough to pay your bills. In John's day, there were lots of soft, low-ante games, but it's an art to find them, and John was an expert at that.

A player needs to visualize the right way to play a game. For example, one great college tennis team starts their season by the players watching films of great tennis players. The coach preps his new players by example. Before they watch films, he throws out his challenge, "Here is the way you're supposed to play. Convert your style to match the masters of the game."

The process of visualization begins with the thought of what it takes to be a professional. A player sees in his mind the image of his ultimate player. If a player visualizes the overall picture of his mistakes, he should be able to adapt his play into a near-perfect style. He mentally converts his game to match his Hero. He buys into the concepts and changes before his next session.

Success occurs when a player consistently plays a more perfect game when he has cured his leaks. If you can't break even, you're missing some concepts, secrets to the game - an edge for winning.

When you finally get to winning, ask yourself, "What does it take for me to play at the next level?"

A player asked John, "John, I usually start off great, but 3 or 4 hours into the session, my play seems to deteriorate. I usually wind up leaving as a loser. I've noticed you usually win. Can you help me out? If not, I think I have to give up poker."

John responded, "Sure! Players are playing better poker than years ago. They've read more books, played more hands, and they collaborate. You come in refreshed. You play good, conservative poker for 3-4 hours, but you start getting a little tired.

Some young-guns come in. They're fresh and they're playing good poker. You need to fight the fatigue off and play better poker than those young-guns. To win, to beat them, you're going to have to tighten up and play more conservatively. You shouldn't play those risky connectors unless you have position where you can limp in on the button. You're not going to win by trying to bluff or double up so you can leave a winner. You have to grind it out and win those small pots. You need patience. You may have to fold bad hands for hours."

That's what I found to be the key to winning. You have to play better and more conservatively as the session goes on. Trying to double-up by bluffing or winning one big hand is a fallacy. Sit there and play better position and better cards. Then, when you win a huge pot and get ahead, or if you sense you're too tired, quit.

It takes decades to learn this lesson, but this strategy is the difference between professionals and also-rans. The common thread is patience and persistence. A professional's play doesn't deteriorate with time. The pro plays better as he learns more about the other players. He plays more conservative and discards his "potential" losing hands.

As you get older, your senses dull faster, so you have to really judge your capabilities and resources. After two or three hours, I have to remind myself, "Okay, you have to play better cards with better position. Don't call with any weak hands, especially when you are out of position."

When you get behind, be patient. Wait for a dealer who will deal you a few winners. It's the same for everything. A great football team will play better in the third and fourth quarters. That's why they win the big games. They put pressure on the other team by using a better strategy. They play more focused in the last quarter.

Position is always the most powerful weapon. "Playing position" refers to playing a poker hand in a higher seat than your opponent. A player in position gets to see the action of an out-of-position [OOP] player before he has to act. After the flop, the dealer has the best "position" because the other players must act before he has to take action.

Position is worth more than one-half of a pot-sized-bet advantage on the river. If I am drawing to a hand and I am OOP, when I hit my draw, it's difficult to effectively bet into a Villain who has position. Any bet from me immediately alerts him that I've improved my hand. To avoid scaring the

Villain, I may check to him even though I hit my nut straight or flush or boat. If I check, I am hoping he will make a bet, preferably a bluff. Of course, if I believe the Villain won't bet, I seize the initiative and bet first.

As it was explained to me by the legendary master of gambling, Mike Svobodny, "If we bet on being able to more closely price an item, and I get to act last, I've got a great advantage. If you say the item is worth $20 and I say it is worth less than $20, I get the benefit of comparing your price to what I think it is worth before I have to respond. You will have given me the range between those values."

If two players have similar skills, the player in position will win. Position does not involve math or odds. As you go from playing fewer hands out of position to playing more hands in position, you reduce your risk, which means you improve your probability of winning.

No charts to memorize, no math to reason about! Having position is more relaxing. There is less guesswork. When you have a quality hand and you get to see the other player's action before you have to commit, you have a tremendous advantage.

Playing after a player with a large stack is a perfect way to start a session, and quitting after you win a big pot is the perfect way to preserve your winnings.

How do you get position? Simple: You cull your hands harder when you are the first to act.

Remember Fritz, the cattle trader in Fayetteville, Texas? Because he had weighed thousands of cattle, he could look at a cow or bull in the field and frequently call the animal's exact weight. Fritz would see a heifer in the field and offer the farmer a price. He simply took the weight and multiplied it by the current price for heifers, minus the profit he wanted to make.

Poker and life are identical. In the game of life, your education, your moral character, and how your associates help you advance is equivalent to position. Opportunities are something you and your mentor need to discuss and analyze. For instance, you should seek expert advice before you commit to a large investment.

A subsequent chapter discusses something I call a marriage-merger. That's the ultimate act of using position. A prominent family leverages their child's future by encouraging them to marry someone with equal or greater potential. Marriage gives the two greater potential because they gain a stronger social position.

A life player may achieve better position by a successful marriage-merger, but he still has to figure out what his opponent has. A player develops patience and proper strategies and as he ages, he has to play more conservative and use position. Position implies you follow the lead of smart people.

Generally speaking, forget about being overly aggressive. It's not a matter of talking yourself into speculating. You will naturally participate more as your game improves. As you play better, you become more aggressive. Sometimes luck plays a role in poker and life. One bad hand can have a devastating effect. Whatever happens, have a great attitude – take the consequences in stride.

Life and poker keep getting more complex. We need to see if we can slow it down and make it less aggressive and more philosophical.

The only question is: How do you win? That's simple – in poker, a player needs to find a soft game he can beat. There was one card-room John played at for over seven years for as long as a month at a time. He never lost. That's hard to believe, but they were soft players, possibly the softest in the U.S.

Would John tell you where this soft card-room is?

How do you win in life? Like John, you learn a skill and find a soft environment where you can be rewarded as you learn the rules and all the tricks. Can you visualize position? That's the game, isn't it?

The Allied nations modernized China by signing one-sided business agreements, but China out-smarted them. China used its position by staying conservative and avoiding the old traps. They didn't give the money back.

Rule 4: Become an expert at playing position. Like China, work with the elites and take their money by patiently playing better position; then, don't give it back

Marriage-mergers and Expectations

A century ago, kids in rural communities were insulated against the outside world. The people surrounding them were ethnically similar, and they cared that everyone in the group had opportunities to advance.

Today, there are more children that suffer from the effects of society. Children are not being taught the proper fundamentals, and they are not brought up in a wholesome environment. Millions of people are on medications, and parents are expected to do more to help children become self-sufficient. As a result, many children don't have an effective support community.

A parent needs to realize that he or she must take it upon themselves to bring their child to a mature level so they can participate in society. That can't be done by telling kids what to do or leaving it up to other groups. Parents need to teach children to make their choices.

If the child's choice is wrong, parents need the patience to allow the child to re-evaluate his or her choice and change his or her mind. Children can only save themselves. Once a parent does this, he enables the child.

This is today's greatest secret and challenge. The simple solution is to talk with your children and let them begin to think on their own. THIS TAKES PATIENCE. Listen until they make the right decision and then just agree.

Once a parent gets the kids where their brains are logically functioning, the parent should start talking about how to succeed early in life. A marriage-merger can be a child's ticket to the future. The marriage-merger is the world's greatest position game; it is an approach to being successful on a long-term basis.

If you marry into it, you don't have to earn it. Old school marriage works. Marriage between wealthy clans is the surest way to come away with the loot, especially if the couple has different sets of knowledge and even if they are from different continents. The marriage-merger is on a scale higher than a good college degree, but the combination of both almost guarantees success. It automatically improves position.

If you read Tilman Fertitta's book *Shut Up And Listen*, it stresses that when he takes a partner in a business deal, he is looking for someone with different knowledge and assets. That's what a marriage-merger is all about and it's the same way with nations and elite groups. That's why Churchill and Roosevelt picked out a group of diverse Allied nations to rule the world.

The movie Titanic was written around a conflict of marrying for love or money and a monster blue stone. If you look at the English nobility, it's the greatest pretend-game in the world. Good-looks help! That was true with Jack and Jackie and it's true for the current heirs to the English throne.

In 1956, Joe Kennedy paid Jackie a million dollars to remain married to Jack. Middle-class America then still wanted the image of romance and fidelity, even if it came at a price. When *Time* printed the story, the Kennedys enlarged the story and used it as publicity. Jackie had supposedly asked for ten million. [Y05]

Jackie decided that if she had enough money and status, she could tolerate Jack's womanizing. She came from a class in which marriages were social and economic opportunities rather than romantic unions. The Auchincloss clan had taught Jackie that it was a get-the-big-money game. Only "commoners" got serious about sex. If you had the big-money there were other entertainment options. [Y06]

The wealthy live in a separate world. The marriage-merger is an effective step to help a family secure a future place at the table. This happens all the time. Two people from wealthy families meet in college. They come from different ethnic clans and different countries. The wealthy Italian Restaurant owner in America sends his daughter to Harvard or

Yale and there she meets and the Jewish son from a wealthy European family that's involved in banking.

Perhaps the wealthy U.S. politician's daughter goes to college in Europe and meets the heir to a French perfume business. There are many wonderful possibilities for sharp young people from upper-class families. The quickest elite merger is a marriage between the potentially rich - for example if they are both doctors. That means a person needs to get the best education possible.

Ivanka Trump's marriage to Jerald Kushner is another example of this formula. A good old Anglo-Catholic girl converts to Judaism and marries a Jewish Orthodox boy. They have mutual interests in power, greed, real estate, politics, and the media. It's a marriage-merger made in heaven.

When we are on the outside looking in, we want in the game. Tell us the rules, and we'll play the game. Sometimes the game is not quite as it seems, or at least it seems different to different people. Oliver Stone said, "I learned nothing from the rich."

Frequently, the upper-class doesn't have as much fun as the middle-class. They live in a bubble. The rich are restricted by their peer groups. They can be a relatively dull club.

Around 1997, I took a scuba diving class in Fort Lauderdale. One of the guys in the class drove a Mercedes and was reputed to be going with the wealthiest lady in Pompano Beach. Between dives, I asked him about his renown.

"Bob, show me a lady who is worth $5M and I'll show you a lady who is looking for a guy with $10M. She has a big boat. The captain takes her out a couple of times a year. It's important to be seen on deck drinking with a nice-looking gentleman as you pass the other boats. You know, they don't know how to have fun like us."

The elites don't go to the restaurants the middle-class frequents. Their kids go to special schools. They enforce a class system, which includes other elites, celebrities, and intellectuals.

The rich travel extensively and eat in four- and five-star restaurants because they don't want to be caught with commoners unless they're slumming. Quoting an insider to the Koch family, "They move in a world with people like them, or who want to be [like them]. They know no poor people at all. They are not the kind of people who feel obligated to get to know the help." [Y07]

One can dabble in the upper-class domain and at the same time take advantage of the fact that a person does not have to live in their dream world. It's nice to mingle with the rich, but most people would rather keep their expectations in check – to stay humble and avoid the elites.

For example, Tony Hillerman won a Pulitzer Prize for his mystery novels set in New Mexico. His books were made into movies. In his autobiography, Hillerman's points out that he was seldom disappointed because he had low expectations. Hillerman loved writing and was content with himself. He didn't miss being able to jet-set around the world.

In contrast, Ted Turner's father wanted to make a million dollars. When he achieved his goal, he quit focusing on making money. He probably went to the country club and played more golf. Ted felt his father lost interest in life, so Ted vowed not to set a limit on the money he might make. Subsequently, Ted made billions, bought a major league baseball team and several big ranches, and married Jane Fonda.

Ted Turner opened a nice club in Bozeman, Montana where one could get a drink and a wonderful buffalo snack.

When I was looking at a horse farm near Bozeman, the owner took me to an exclusive restaurant outside of Bozeman that required reservations. Ted Turner owned a hundred-thousand acre ranch in the area. One day Ted and Jane showed up at this restaurant without reservations and they were denied service.

My expectations were small, and I enjoyed a fine meal with the thought that I was seated and Ted and Jane weren't. I savored smug anti-jealousy.

Rule 5: Help your children become decision-makers. Allow them to analyze situations and make their decisions. Teach them to think about the early advantages in education and marriage. This strategy will have many rewards, but it takes patience on your part to engineer.

Everything Evolves

In 1832, as Texas settlers arrived, Fredrick Ernst wrote back to friends in Europe about the Austin Colony: "The ground is hilly and alternates with natural grass plains. Various kinds of trees; climate like that of Sicily. The soil needs no fertilizer. Almost constant east wind. No winter. Almost like March in Germany. … Wild prey such as deer, bears, raccoons, wild turkey, geese, partridge (as large as domestic fowls) in quantity. Free hunting and fishing. Wild horses and buffaloes in herds. … Scarcely three months of work a year."

"No need for money, free exercise of religion, and the best markets for all products at the Mexican harbors; up river there is much silver, but there are still Indian races there. We men satisfy ourselves with hunting and horse racing."

In some places, the grass grew as tall as a man's chest. Another settler wrote that in a twenty-mile journey a rider could see a thousand to two thousand deer.

The Austin Colony was between two great rivers, the Colorado and the Brazos; that meant the land had groundwater, and small farmers could work the land.

To the south and west, the environment was drier and more suited for ranches; Richard King and the Olivers chose to establish large ranches in that harsher environment.

Mr. Robert Oliver II died in December 2019. The service was held at the Cinco Ranch Church of Christ in Katy, Texas.

The deceased Robert Oliver's father was an authority on cattle and a judge. He was one of three judges when the King estate divided the herd on King Ranch.

When Oliver was growing up, his father was in charge of examining cattle in Mexico for hoof and mouth disease. The family would spend a month out of the year in Mexico.

It's all a small world. Robert Oliver met John Wayne when Wayne was filming a movie in Mexico. When he was taking military training in California, he called up Wayne on the set, and Wayne fixed him and his buddy up with dates with starlets.

Oliver's father was an expert on operating large ranches and hunting preserves. He managed a ranch with over 400,000 acres in Mexico. Richard King III might fly in with Lloyd Benson and his father. The Olivers attracted that type of company at the big ranch.

I had written a chapter on Oliver in *JFK and the World Oligarchy*. My book was on display with three other books, Oliver's boots, and his hand-made Montecristi hat. Two of the books on display were written by Oliver. One was how to fly undetected into all the airports in South America.

I was glad to see my book on display. I'd never asked Oliver's opinion as to the accuracy of my chapter on him. I wrote Mr. Oliver up as one of the world's great assassins and a brave soldier, but I wondered if I'd been too harsh with my characterization of him. Being on display, signified my book had validity.

I asked Oliver's daughter where the replica spurs were, the ones that were a copy of those his uncle gave to Pancho Villa.

"They were too hard to get out of the case they were mounted in."

Several Oliver families were early Texas ranchers – big ranchers. In the early 1900s, a member of one of the old Oliver families gave an expensive set of spurs to Pancho Villa. He was a friend of Pancho.

Oliver was with Pancho one day and they were distantly watching U.S. troops commanded by John J. Pershing. The U.S. had invaded Mexico to put down border violence. Pancho handed Oliver his viewing scope and asked if he knew the scout with Pershing. Oliver replied, "Yes, he's my cousin."

The next day, Oliver took a train back to the U.S. border. When he arrived, the newspaper carried the news that

Pancho Villa had crossed the border on the prior day and raided ranches in New Mexico. That wasn't true. Villa's army couldn't move that far that quickly. Yes, there was fake news even back then!

When Pershing was reassigned to Europe for WW I, Pancho was again free to roam. Pancho gave Oliver a letter stating he could move cattle and horses anywhere in Pancho's territory without being interfered with.

One day, when Oliver was moving four to five hundred head of cattle, he was robbed of his herd. The next time Oliver saw Pancho, Pancho asked how he was doing. Oliver told Pancho about the robbery. When Pancho asked who did it, he said, "One of your men. He's right over there."

Oliver pointed the man out and Pancho asked his officer to come over to talk. Pancho asked him if he had robbed Oliver. When he admitted it, Pancho shot and killed him. If Pancho hadn't killed his officer, it would have sent a message to others that officers could ignore his word.

A man's word was his bond. If you didn't live up to it, you couldn't be a leader of the group. You might get killed. That's why there was honesty among thieves. They had rules like everyone else. That is true throughout society. That's why people say, "Just tell me the rules so I can play the game." That's also why the sheep aren't taught the rules, so they can't play the game.

Pancho told Oliver he would have a like number of cattle delivered to a particular border city nine days later within an hourly time range.

The nice thing about those days was that all the transactions were for cash. I'm sure little of the revenue was reported. That's why a great sheriff like Wild Bill Hickock was charged with collecting taxes; he could make the equivalent of one million dollars a year.

Cash transactions are interesting. I was working in Freeport, Maine on a contract for UNUM. I heard that the only good BBQ place in Maine gave a discount for cash purchases. I asked about it, and it was the same as the Maine sales tax, about 7 percent.

The early Texas oil businesses lived by an honor code. If you were doing seismic processing, a company like Humble Oil & Refining might ship your company some data without an order. Your company would just have Humble's word. If your seismic company needed money, you had to hope the banker would believe you had unbilled work but no documents to back it up.

"My word is my bond" has changed with the advent of point of sale terminals and databases. Everything has to be quickly verifiable. The customer-order table needs an entry of the purchase order number and for management to look ahead, work-in-process is important. The days of Pancho Villa stories and the absence of a purchase-order number are gone.

Do you remember the fabulous cars with big chrome bumpers that got 11 miles to the gallon on leaded gasoline? I bought a new 1967 teal GTO convertible, the prettiest car I had ever seen, for around $3300. We were so lucky back then, but that was when virginity started to disappear.

About that time, a set of new apartments in Dallas offered renters a free round-trip to Acapulco one year after signing their lease. Those apartments rented out quickly. A year later, the president of our computer company [Tom Toland at NCS] went on the Acapulco trip.

On the journey, Tom met a lady from Dallas who was also taking advantage of the free trip. The morning they were scheduled to return, Tom asked her for her phone number. She smiled and politely replied, "We've had a wonderful time, but I'll be a different girl when I get back to Dallas."

In 1969, our computer company, National Computer Service, acquired the John Squires Company. Mr. Squires' company did the integration of oil well charts that were used to measure the production flowing from wells into pipelines. There wasn't anything radical we could do to improve Squires' business. It was more than a decade before microprocessor chips would find their way into doing flow measurement.

We were going to be a go-go computer company. We were going to buy companies and raise money and go public and make a million dollars on paper as quickly as possible, and it worked. Past that point, the stockholders or investors, the real dreamers, were on their own.

Mr. Squires was in his late 50s and our group was in our 20s. After we had finalized our business discussions, Mr. Squires shared some personal information with us. His daughter had moved in with a man. He was quite concerned. Here we were, young guys chasing young ladies, but because we appeared as businessmen in suits, John didn't grasp that we were on the other side of the equation.

Unmarried sex became so popular virginity disappeared in less than a decade. The older people had the hardest time understanding, especially fathers.

To young men, virginity became a non-event. People may have a hard time believing this, but sex became part of the first or second date. If not, there might not be a third date.

We weren't thinking about virgins. If we met one, she was soon off our list. And, we weren't interested in moving in with someone either. Life was too good.

The U.S. middle-class was peaking and in 1971 President Richard Nixon was forced to take the U.S. off the gold standard. Free sex and Nixon action were signs of things to come. Greed would later cause the use of drugs to take hold.

One year my son Michael asked. "Do you think I should play baseball this summer or work?"

"Play! You're going to work for 50 years, and the window to play baseball is small."

It's important for younger people to participate in sports. People normally find a sport boring if they haven't played. Non-players miss the implications of the actions.

For instance, I attended an Astros game and the opposing team's manager walked out of the dugout after a pitch. He went to first base and said something to their runner. Then, the runner was lifted and another was put in to replace him.

A team manager rarely leaves the dugout to talk with a player on first base. I said to the people with me, "The manager gave the runner a signal to steal second, but he didn't. The manager just asked the runner if he saw the signal. When the runner acknowledged he had seen the signal, he got replaced."

No one said anything. They didn't understand baseball well enough to comment. I had an opinion because I had played as a pitcher and a catcher.

On the next pitch, the new runner tried to steal second and was thrown out. That was my confirmation.

Football and basketball, being team sports, are harder to analyze. They are less boring because of the action of every play.

Golf is worse. A spectator must analyze the physical talents and mind control of a golfer.

To a golfer, it takes courage to chip a golf ball onto the green. It also takes a precise feel to glide a putt from 30 feet to up next to the hole. If you haven't played golf, you can't appreciate the mixture of skill and fear that occupies one's mind.

When I was an active golfer shooting 100 in a round, I thought of giving up the game, but instead, I bought a new set of clubs. In the set was a driver with a huge head. I discovered I could knock the ball a long way. It took three or four strokes off my game and gave me more confidence. As I mastered the use of the rest of my clubs, my game worked its way down to the mid-80s, bogey golf.

It helps to move into a subdivision next to three relatively inexpensive golf courses. On any nice day, I could ride across the street and play. I became a content golfer.

A half a dozen years went by, and there were a couple of big floods in Houston. Two nearby courses closed down and many of my playing buddies got too old. I kept the clubs and the memories. The hole in one and the eight birdies in a round keep me coming back, like the old man who had once won the big poker tournament. I still have those swings grooved in my mind.

Like golf, I love the outdoors, especially fishing. Fishing is like finding that big golf driver. When the fish are hitting every lure you cast, it's not the fish that are hooked; you're hooked. You remember a few stories of the big ones that did and didn't get away.

Southern society has a blank spot between the end and start of football season. I told my friend Jay Pollard, "Now football is over. I've run out of things to watch. I've seen the significant movies. Television is only good for a few events and current information, but there's not much there. Things have started to be boring."

Jay summarized in a word, "Books!"

There is wonderful information in books, and there is a vast dictionary called the Internet.

I had stopped at Barnes & Noble the day before. I browsed hurriedly and wrote down three titles – *How to do Nothing*, *Fake*, and *A Traitor to His Race*. I went home and checked the comments out on Amazon. *A Traitor to His Race* had great reviews. It was an older book on Franklin Roosevelt that could be purchased used from Amazon for less than $3, plus shipping. Such a deal!

Amazon has destroyed book stores and the publishing industry. We are in a cycle where the malls we used to love are being destroyed. I know because I love bookstores and I walk in malls.

Capitalism is pervasive. First, we had urbanization and the town square. Then Wal-Mart became the town-square killer. Now we have Amazon, the most cannibalistic.

After 1970, things changed slowly, but to men, it was always about sports, games, the outdoors, friends, and family.

How do sports relate to the coming digital age? Simple! Our games and sports will change just like sports went from horse racing to football in the last 200 years. Everything gradually changes. What makes football is sports-betting. There are so many games, one can waste the whole weekend.

Although the early settlers found what they were looking for, people are still coming. Bastrop, Texas, a town between LaGrange and Austin, is projected to grow 25% in 2020 and 400% by 2030. The reason for Bastrop's growth is that Austin has its expansion blocked to the north.

Those growth figures were on the table before Tesla announced they would build a large plant between Austin and Bastrop. The growth forecast will probably double, but I won't applaud because there are too many people. More people will turn more of the land into solar farms, taxes will go up, and the traffic is already bad.

Future growth of Houston, Dallas, Austin, and San Antonio will overpower the small county seats of what made up the Austin Colony. Fayetteville will be like Los Gatos in Silicon Valley, at the end of a thread, flapping in the winds of change, a place where people come to drink a beer or eat barbecue or have a kolache. Those visitors will think of hills or bays or distant points to feel removed from civilization, although they will be a mere 20 minutes from an entry ramp of a freeway.

The old Austin Colony has outstanding chicken fried steaks with cream gravy and tremendous brisket barbecue, the kind Snow's in Lexington and Franklin's in Austin serve. Snow's is number one in Texas and Franklin's is number two.

Prause Meat Market in LaGrange had great brisket and pork, but their specialty was sausage, perhaps the best in the U.S. There is a tremendous amount of great sausage in the far north from Boston to Chicago, but I have never met a Yankee who thought they had better sausage. [Prause closed down in

2020 and sold their business. The new operation is scheduled to reopen on Highway 71.]

Not to disparage other BBQ places, but the Texas barbecue is comparable to Joe's in Kansas City. Great BBQ is sometimes defined by the length of the waiting line. The currency is brisket, sausage, ribs, or pork, and the choices are Snow's, Franklin's, Luling, Mikeska, Goode, Spring Creek, Rudy's, and other places, like the BBQ places in Lockhart.

Luling has the best ribs in the world, so from LaGrange, one has access to the best BBQ in the world. I have named the local establishments, but Killen has a gourmet steak and BBQ near Houston that is out of this world.

I'll stick to the locals. You might try BBQ Inn for chicken fried steak, chicken, BBQ, and seafood. They are at Yale and Crosstimbers in Houston.

The Bushes were experts on fishing and BBQ. When I fished the Salmon River in upstate New York, H.W. was in there at the peak of the season a week before I arrived. And when I fished for tarpon and bonefish in the Keys, my guide spoke of H.W.

When I did a software contract for Certified Vacations in Fort Lauderdale, a friend invited me to go to the Elk's Club in Pompano Beach where Jeb Bush was chasing votes. Jeb was having a barbecue dinner for potential voters. A BBQ dinner given by a candidate means a grilled hamburger with an onion ring.

When everything had been said, and people backed off, I asked Jeb, "Is there anything like Otto's here in Florida?"

At Otto's in Houston, they had a Bush platter that was to die for - great brisket, sausage, and everything. When H.W. Bush was president and he wanted BBQ catered, he called Otto's, Goode Company, or Luther's.

Without a blink, Jeb said, "No, there's nothing like Otto's in Florida. I usually go to Shorty's at Dadeland and U.S. 1 [in Miami]."

I didn't tell Jeb that Tom's on Federal in Lauderdale was one of the better BBQ places in Florida. I tried Shorty's a few days later and he was right; it was marginal.

Innovations drive social changes. Today, most people don't know their neighbors. When people didn't have automobiles, they had time to visit with neighbors.

The kings and queens are almost gone. The English Royals appear antiquated. Perhaps they will have the conscience to gracefully end their dumb charade.

Like a bird seeing the shadow of a hawk, we have survival DNA in our genes. As we get older, we avoid conflict - perhaps we even lie to ourselves.

In 1931, Albert Einstein wrote his world views in an essay. He concluded, "It is my conviction that killing under the cloak of war is nothing but an act of murder."

After Einstein was hired for a teaching job at Stanford, he surely tempered his focus when the Allied military initiated war strategies.

The United States has been lucky. The digital age began in 2000 with the first large databases. Now companies use powerful software to get answers. In the future, everything will be quicker and easily solvable. This breakthrough should be great, but we have no technocrat leaders - just greedy elites in control.

American workers are trapped. They were in a hurry going in an unfocused direction with no goals, destroying the environment, and accomplishing very little. Workers were panning for gold, but they hadn't sampled the sub-surface to see if there were any deposits. Now, they may be destroyed in the new digital world unless the system is changed.

The public has an opportunity for the first time in history to do away with all of the overhead. The public won't need religions, the Deep State, fake news, mafias, and non-productive structures. Nations need to restrain population growth and minimize the use of resources.

The planet needs to reorganize resources. A large population means wages will go to subsistence. The world needs everyone to do simple and productive functions. Families could use renewable energy sources and work from home.

If society was optimally organized, the public would have more quality time. If nations reduced the required work by 70%, life would become more like Fredrick Ernst wrote, "Scarcely three months of work a year. No need for money."

We are now stuck in a grinding mode. Voltaire was also correct when he stated, "The art of government consists of taking as much money as possible from one [middle] class to give to another [the establishment]."

The United States' major issues never get addressed because the elites maintain a static social structure. They make sure the oligarchs' fiat money, patents, and banking systems remain in control. The elites do this by using a Supreme Court that doesn't allow changes. A flexible system would encourage the public to redo the banking system, SCOTUS, and the Constitution. Transparency is natural in the digital age. This should be discussed and brought about by Congress.

When Ron Paul was a Congressman, he wanted FED transparency, but he couldn't deliver. At the time, society wasn't capable of implementing transparency, but the digital age offers an easy conversion to transparency. The books can be opened quickly. The public could immediately see the tax returns and who stole all the money! Of course, the oligarchs will try to stop the public from looking at their books.

The threat of a power shift has caused the oligarchs to install restrictive forms of control. The liberal Democrats profess to want the public's guns. That means they want the sheep controlled like they are in England.

This is all in support of the oligarchs, people like the Rockefellers. The wealthy conservatives can't allow the bankers at Mellon, J.P. Morgan, HSBC, Union, BOE, and Lloyds to be put under the microscope.

It would help if everyone agreed it would be to their benefit to include the open-minded sheep in their power groups. Transparency should be encouraged by the media and Congress. Instead, the public condones a series of great lies. The public needs to retool the political parties and replace politicians with thinkers.

In 2020, institutional racism almost caused a coup. Racism is not going away. It's impossible to have Congress consider this issue; the GOP and the Jews and the Catholics have racist platforms. You don't see African Americans in bed with them. Take the clue. Certain clans are racist.

When Rob Rosenstein was deputy attorney general in 2018, there were 115,000 employees in the Department of Justice. Rosenstein was Jewish and the Jewish Syndicate is the most racist and clannish, and those groups are arrogant and collusive, like mafias. That is a major problem because the United States needs non-racist leaders.

Sammy Habeeb, a world-class expert on dice and casino operation, told me, "I just need an edge."

When you give a clannish group an edge, they want more. Religions and mafias are that way, but our government doesn't need bias. It needs balance and a longer-term perspective. Perhaps, the clannish groups should be proportioned by population, or something like the slot-limit used to control the bass and flounder populations.

Rule 6: Remain neutral in politics. Be politically correct, and for the good of the world, systemic racism and clannish bias need to be minimized. The world needs to look into the future and implement better plans. Social change needs to be intelligently engineered.

We don't need oligarchs' sucking off profits and taking advantage of the uneducated sheep. We need to fix the system by lowering the population and educating everyone to where we share the same big picture. This is not that complex. Even a country boy can understand this.

Technology's Pervasiveness

In the 1960s, companies like Electronic Data Systems went public and made people like Ross Perot billionaires. The lure of success drew software developers into the venture market. Sweat equity in the form of an option on the corporate stock was the attraction.

A stock option was normally for letter stock, which might not be immediately tradable on the open markets. By the time the people receiving the sweat-equity option had the right to sell their stock to the public, the value of the stock may have fallen by a considerable amount.

After the roaring 1960s, the computer market settled back to the status quo before the microcomputer revolution offered a glimmer of life. I worked on projects which developed messaging systems using embedded code on micros. I wrote code for almost every private-line communication protocol in existence.

The data processing world was yet to be connected to the Internet. Message communications were on a separate network. There was no integrated personal messaging - no emails and no cell phones. Society was just beginning to use credit cards, and data processing managers were not concerned about the prospect of outsiders stealing information.

I was with Lane Telecommunications and we shipped a messaging system to the J.P. Morgan bank in New York. The system sent and received Telex, TWX, and DDD messages. It was supposed to automatically print out any incoming foreign-transfer requests. Those requests for funds came in as Telex messages. The volumes weren't big, but the dollars were substantial.

One system we shipped had an error. J.P. Morgan noticed the problem and we replaced the system. The bank simply sent a message to their correspondents telling them that if they had sent wire instructions in the last few days to resend them.

That's how casual the big money transactions were. There was no need for security because the communications were between a small number of large business clients. Life was less stressful in the old days.

The same type of system Lane shipped to J.P. Morgan was sent to Coastal Corporation, an energy company run by Oscar Wyatt. Coastal's system was put on an international barge transporting crude to a Texas refinery. When the ship was unloaded, the receiving facility couldn't take the entire load. The crew tried to communicate with other refiners along the Galveston ship channel to see if they would take the remainder, but they didn't get any replies since the Lane system wasn't properly printing all incoming messages.

The Coastal vessel dumped the rest of the crude, a small amount, in the ocean before it went back for another load. Slightly later, Coastal discovered the problem. The Coastal CEO, Oscar Wyatt, was livid and wanted to sue, but since Coastal had dumped the crude in our clean ocean, Oscar couldn't pursue this issue.

I knew of Oscar Wyatt. When I was with IBM, I helped develop Sakowitz's first computer installation. Sakowitz was a small, luxury department-store chain in Houston. The downtown Sakowitz store had a wonderful dining area on the top floor. When I came back for a visit, the systems group invited me to lunch. Small events like that are what people remember.

Bernard Sakowitz was the Sakowitz CEO, and Oscar Wyatt paid Bernard a million dollars for his daughter Lynn's hand. Lynn would sometimes stop at corporate when she bought furs in Russia for the Sakowitz stores.

Sakowitz's controller was Irv Weiner. Irv spoke four languages, graduated from Rutgers, and was head of Houston's Retail Merchants' Association. Irv's big thing was "cost of sales." That's where you distribute the overall cost back to each item to determine if you are making a profit on the items you sell. Irv went to the detail level so he knew where the money was being made or lost.

In the 1990s, companies began connecting their messaging systems to their data processing systems so their corporate management could message their remote branches, and vice-versa. The technology was changing, but managers had little reason to be concerned if someone was going to copy some code or steal data because there was no access from the outside world and the absence of databases restricted meaningful results.

Operating system code was written in assembler, which was specific to the machine's language. The software wasn't quickly convertible to a different set of hardware because general languages like Pascal and C weren't used.

The core software needed speed and efficiency. Hardware was relatively slow and very expensive. This limited the amount of hardware that was used and the scope of projects. Machine language was more memory efficient, and many times we developed systems that used all of the memory.

During the mid-1990s, the Internet was used to occasionally send a short message to a specific person or to browse a URL offering risqué jokes. News, social networks, financial information, and large databases were yet to appear.

I did some work in Silicon Valley for Sytek in Mountain View. Sytek developed broadband products. I managed the development of a system to handle bisynchronous packet data. I beta-tested at Lawrence Livermore where Sytek had installed a 25-megabit broadband line to handle the cross-campus communications.

I also managed a Sytek project to develop a secure network product. It would have been marketed to intelligence agencies or law enforcement groups. Sytek must have gotten me a security clearance, but I don't remember hearing of one.

The same was probably true when I worked at NASA for IBM. Pre-2000, security was a casual happening. The people validating clearances may have said, "Here's a good-old-white-boy who hasn't been arrested. We can stamp him with a lower level clearance." They didn't parse Internet social history because there was none.

In the late-1990s, databases were a new approach to storing data and accessing records. Following the money trail, I shifted my skill-set and focused on working for large commercial customers with database conversion requirements. Databases eliminated the Y2K type of date problems by making the year four digits instead of two. This caused firms to push through database conversions prior to 2000.

One of my last jobs of this type was a conversion with Andersen Consulting for American Express in Florida. I was a Subject Matter Expert on databases and commercial software. I did the QA on some software conversions by the TATA Group in India, and I managed some conversions in Mexico and Brazil. I was assigned a beautiful Portuguese translator.

The effort to avoid the 2000 date rollover problem superseded the integration of secure systems, but after 2000 security became an issue because cell phones and personal computers began to be connected to corporate networks. This forced the integration of the Internet.

When Y2K concluded, commercial software jobs on the job site Dice plummeted from 180,000 jobs to less than 30,000. After 9-11, military jobs were in demand.

Moore's law implied memory speed should double every 18 months. Miniaturization of hardware and enhanced speed of networks caused the integration of message communications, commercial data centers, and scientific computer systems.

With the unleashing of more powerful microcomputers, the virtual world began to appear. Minicomputer manufacturers, like Digital Equipment, Data General, and Wang, began to lose market share as microprocessor systems became competitive. In two decades, micros and the virtual social world took control.

In the 2000-2010 timeframe, the old Telex messaging systems Lane Telecommunications supplied to banks were replaced by secure systems that were robust and scalable. The

Society for Worldwide Interbank Telecommunications, SWIFT, was the messaging system that became a centerpiece for handling U.S. international banking transactions. Now, another system is being offered by the Chinese.

Hardly anyone notices the software changes. The virtual world seeps in, and when a person looks back a couple of years later, there it is. In the 1990s, H. Ross Perot was right when he suggested a Congressman could work from his home by using video conferencing. By 2022, rather than sleeping in his Washington office, a Congressman should be able to work from his home computer room. The state and federal government need to put this in their budgets.

Ever since our nation was founded, the elites have built walls to contain technical people, and the politicians maintain the walls.

The Deep Stators, parading with security clearances, are not about security. They are a society of usurpers - well-paid pawns who want to control technology so they can help the oligarchs play their one-world game.

The public gives Congressmen and government representatives too much credit for understanding technology. Very few in Washington are qualified to discuss the technical influences of our new virtual society.

A closed perspective persisted for Congressmen on any committee for the military. John McCain, Diane Feinstein, and Lindsey Graham were basically non-productive since 2000. They were military spokespeople who offered few solutions - zombies who said what their supporters wanted to hear.

Politicians aren't qualified to explain why the Supreme Court and the Constitution are not designed for a technical society. Technical ignorance carries through all government agencies, Congress, and the White House.

Electing Donald Trump to drain the swamp was fiction. Trump became the center of the swamp. Trump's instinctive queries were, "Does it make money? Can I participate?"

John Bolton concluded Trump "couldn't tell the difference between his personal interests and the country's interest." [Y08]

After Bolton released his book, every Republican I asked about Bolton's quote would go into an analysis of why Bolton was incompetent. Until Bolton sold Trump out, Democrats regarded him as the enemy, but now Bolton is kind of a hero to the Democrats. That shows how polarization can quickly flip to adoration or condemnation.

If you are an open-minded person, you know politicians will not restore the middle-class. The effects of technology are too complex for real technical issues to ever be discussed in the West Wing. That group only understands how to underpay, ignore, and lay off top technical people.

In the corporate world, business executives are just as bad. They speak in management, marketing, business, and political terms. Their focus is on their business plan. Their relationship with the technical staff is: "Give me the product. I want to broadly communicate with the manager of computer systems. The people below the manager are nerds. Who cares about software? I'm someone important."

An executive wouldn't be hired by a corporate board if he didn't have a software deficiency. Society and boards of most corporations are not concerned with the digital age. In 2018, Japan's new cybersecurity minister admitted he never used a computer. He should have been "thrown under the bus."

The masses find their level early in life. They fail to grasp how to improve their lot, but great leaders rise in status because they are so correct that people step aside and listen in respect for their opinions. Leaders have patience and are lucky - in the right place at the right time with the right support.

Politicians are naturally born liars and represent a special case. To verify their greatness, our leaders need to be required to submit to a battery of tests. Lie-detector tests need to be included.

Rule 7: Take responsibility. Dress accordingly; associate with elites and show them you can make decisions. Be good for your word. Strive to provide leadership.

Very closely evaluate politicians. Try to find the biggest liar you feel comfortable in supporting, but avoid your macho instincts. Demand an intelligent voice.

Racism, Imperialism, and Exceptionalism

Intellectuals speak in terms of states, nations, or nation-states. They avoid the real power centers. A nation is like a molecule containing atoms, where the atoms are the elite groups. Those groups are clannish, and they control what a nation-state does.

Although they represent separate clans, the elites are bonded by their attraction to power. This bonding makes the nation-state more powerful, but ultimately these groups of elites encounter a stalemate. Each seeks a monopoly of power, and this forces them to form larger and more rigid alliances.

My Theory:

"As technology advanced and the world population increased, wars led to a consolidation of power as rules-based societies were pitted against aggressive rulers."

"Since the end of WW II, the Allied elites have focused on creating a one-world society. Now they have been forced to enter a dangerous new phase of their Grand Area strategy."

Wars are initiated because of greed, racism, necessity, vision, and ego.

Racism and the egotistical desire for power are building blocks for social conflicts and world power. Racism surfaces in clans of different color, language, size, and intellect. Conflicts may be inherited. One family may grow up hating another family, or as one family traverses the land it meets another family with a desirable asset.

Within a clan's DNA is some weird macho desire for power or recognition or ownership. For example, racism dominated the settling of the West. The American settlers were escaping the bonds of poverty and war in Europe. Free land meant a ticket to the middle-class. Anglos couldn't let "savages" stand in their way.

George Washington, Abraham Lincoln, and Franklin Roosevelt set a gold standard for leadership in the United States and Winston Churchill did the same on the other side of the pond for the English.

Franklin Roosevelt thought at an international level, and like Churchill, he was a grand schemer. Roosevelt was a New York lawyer. As a young man, he loved sailing and belonged to all of the best clubs. He was athletic and played golf before he caught polio.

Roosevelt's uncle Delano made his fortune as an opium smuggler in China. Franklin Roosevelt could be considered European. He was well-traveled. Roosevelt spent much of his early life in Europe. His accent wasn't American. It was more of an English accent.

Near the end of WW II, Churchill encouraged Roosevelt to go with him to Marrakech, Morocco, and view the sunset on the snows of the Atlas Mountains. They saw the dimming light paint the snowy peaks with shifting pastels.

The next day as Roosevelt's plane lifted, Churchill said to his driver as they left separately, "If anything happened to that man, I couldn't stand it. He is the truest friend; he has the farthest vision; he is the greatest man I have ever known." [Y09] To me, that sounds too scripted.

H.W. Brands' book, *Traitor to His Class*, has a tremendous portrait of Franklin Roosevelt's life and career. Brand's masterpiece also reflects on the character and intellectualism of Joseph Stalin as well as the adversarial nature of the relationships between the warring nations - Germany, England, Russia, U.S., Japan, China, Italy, France, etc. You will come away with the thought that Stalin was intelligent and understood the rest of the world.

The Russians initially lost millions of troops because Stalin was slow to react to warnings by Churchill. That may have been because Stalin was very suspicious of the Anglo association. He thought that behind his back there was an unfair connection between the United States and England by Roosevelt and Churchill.

When you review WW II and the Grand Area plans, Stalin was correct. The Russians suffered the loss of millions of troops partially because Roosevelt and Churchill were slow to open a second front. This allowed the Russian troops to rape and pillage, but that may have been the Allied plan; Churchill and Roosevelt may have thought they needed a strong future adversary. War is never a perfect science.

At the end of WW II, the Allied nations gave Russia the better of the deal. They gave Russia half of Germany and part of Europe. That agreement may have been made to enlarge the Russian presence in order to march the world into a static wall for the next 75 years. The Allied elites needed a vile opponent to build their world-class military, and the threat of communism replaced Nazism as the adversary.

It's difficult to discuss famous people with a dual-edged knife. It's easy to only mention good things about Winston Churchill, but Churchill admitted he was a pawn of the British cabal, the powerful oligarchs who defined the Allied nations' future. Churchill bowed to the Rothschild clan and they had a history of scheming to take advantage of nations.

The English cabal was composed of the masters. They could never be trusted. That's old history, but rumors persist. Some of my philosophical friends believe the English cabal is still not to be trusted.

As food for thought, Stalin thought Churchill had Roosevelt poisoned. Churchill was Cecil Rhodes' disciple and Rhodes had worked with de Beers and Rothschild. Churchill may have had a darker side, or the British oligarchs could have poisoned Roosevelt at Marrakech.

Whatever level of schemer the English might be, Stalin's whole mind-concept of communism was that of a revolutionary. Stalin sought total domination of everyone. If he had to kill everyone to do that, that would be Stalin's solution. Stalin was a sorry, worthless Pol Pot.

The post-WW II period was a time of enormous evolution, a time when Winston Churchill spoke privately of the elites, or as he referred to them, a "High Cabal" that made us what we are. [Y10]

Deceased playwright Arthur Miller, the author of The Misfits and former husband of Marilyn Monroe, said, "Those who formally rule take their signals and commands, not from the electorate as a body, but from a small group…"

"This group will be called the establishment. It exists, even though that existence is starkly denied; it is one of the secrets of the American social order."

Like Winston Churchill, Arthur Miller never named the elites. Miller warned against discussing them, adding, "People are not allowed to speak of the establishment."

Churchill and Roosevelt were of the old elite class and felt sure they were endowed to run the world. They came from an era when marriage among the rich was for money and power. Jack Kennedy was of Irish blood and of a similar background.

The Anglophiles and the Native Americans had communication problems besides inherent racism. John Wayne expressed his thoughts by saying, "Our so-called stealing this country from Indians was just a matter of survival. There were great numbers of people who needed new land, and the Indians were selfishly trying to keep it for themselves."

["Sure, the only good Indian is a dead Indian. Don't give them the Black Hills with the gold. Throw them a little rancid meat and a treaty! Lie to those savages."]

Perception and nearness facilitate racism. China will trade with the U.S. at arm's length, but that's as far as it goes.

I met an expert on antique rugs. When he was younger, he flew into China to buy antiquities. His work bordered on shady business. One day a Chinese gentleman asked him, "Do you know who those men are, the ones that moved in across the street?"

When he acknowledged they were strangers, the gentleman confided, "They're Russian. They were brought in to kill you. If I were you, I wouldn't be here tonight."

The antiquities buyer picked up a few things, went out to his plane, and flew out of China.

Louis Lesser, told me a similar story. Lesser was one of the largest builders in the U.S. in the 1950s and 1960s. When he was building Barrington Plaza in California, he called up President Jack Kennedy and said, "I'm running into problems. I need an additional $100M FHA loan."

Jack replied, "Come to Washington and talk to me." Lesser did, and his loan was forthcoming.

Decades later, when Lesser was in a home for the elderly, a relative of his asked me to review her uncle's long list of assets to see if there was anything salvageable. I was interested. Lesser had done deals with Howard Hughes. He was with Robert Kennedy when Robert was killed. He placed his hand on Robert's chest as he lay on the floor.

When Lesser's Barrington Plaza development was completed, his company had $100M in cash reserves. He placed his company in the hands of his children before he and his wife moved to China for five years.

Mr. Lesser was an aggressive developer. In his businesses, he probably offended a few of the locals. After five years, one day a Chinese friend told Louis, "They're going to kill you if you are still here this evening."

Mr. Lesser immediately collected his wife and they took the first plane out of China. They packed nothing. And when they got back to the U.S., the Lessers discovered the kids had given themselves bonuses. The $100M in assets had vanished. Five years is a long time.

The Chinese are not partial to foreigners who want to make a quick buck. Why? First, there is a difference in skin color. It would be okay if a foreigner brought money and left quickly after he or she had spent the money.

The same attitude exists in the U.S. Mainers advertise their state as a vacationland on car license plates, which is a polite way of saying, "Bring money, spend it, and then leave Maine. This is our territory. Lobster fishing is a local industry. We don't want the competition."

Foreigners hate imperialists, and Americans top their list. I met a young man who was about to graduate from a prestigious U.S. college. He had spent three years in Japan and spoke fluent Japanese. I asked him if he considered returning to Japan to work in some type of international business. He said, "No, they hate us."

This young student went on to describe how he had taken a bus and the Japanese man across the aisle said to the other riders in their native language, "Look at this foreign trash riding the bus with us."

A large number of Japanese regard foreigners as non-slant-eyed opportunists. They may never get past the atomic bombs, the U.S. occupation, or the U.S.'s monetary games.

Racism sometimes exists between two nations whose borders touch. For example, in 1976, Jimmy Carter brought Menachem Begin and Anwar Sadat together at Camp David for thirteen days of peace talks. They wasted the first three days with arguments. Carter then separated Begin and Sadat and negotiated with them separately. Carter realized Begin and Sadat hated each other's country. [That agreement cost Sadat his life.]

In the 1990s, I was sitting with a small group at a house in Silicon Valley. The young sheik from Kuwait asks, "What do you think of Israel?"

"I don't have an opinion. What do you think?"

"I think we should kill them all. But, why don't you have an opinion?"

"Well, I've never lived next to them [or Arabian people]. If I did, I might have an opinion."

The Jewish people and Arabs are polarized, but the hatred is not just Jews versus Muslims. In September of 2015, al Qaeda leader Al-Zawahiri declared war on ISIS leader Abu Bakr al-Baghdadi. It may take centuries for power groups in the Middle East to peacefully co-exist. This "hate" is a result of different religious beliefs and conflicting centers of power.

Racism separates clans, which are effectively mafias, self-serving ethnic groups. Therefore, laws against racism are contrary. Racism is here to stay - inherent and universal. In the red-necked, white, male crowd, expect anti-female and anti-other-ethnic-clan racism.

Americans have extreme racism and the best of the best. Besides racism, Americans and Europeans, and particularly the English, have been societies whose social structure and goals were superior. For instance, Europeans had centuries to perfect their society. They taught their children a more refined social approach.

When the Europeans colonized other continents, the native Indians and African Americans were forced to adapt their rules and beliefs. Teddy Roosevelt hypothesized it might take a century or two for an "uncivilized" society to transition to the Anglo social system.

Imperialism was in place long before the discovery of the New World, but after Columbus' discovery and Magellan's voyage proved the world was round, the focus of world power abruptly changed. England, France, Russia, Spain, Italy,

Germany, Japan, Portugal, and the Netherlands realized the world was a sphere, and therefore landmass was finite.

Walter Prescott Webb referred to the fifteenth-century imperialist nations as the Metropolis. The Metropolis elites theorized the world would be controlled by the nations who colonized the most and the best land. The aggressive nations immediately sent fleets of explorers to find treasure and claim land.

No eloquent speech could have altered the taming of the West. Colonization was a brutal racist attitude. It allowed a nation to forcefully acquire the property of a technically inferior clan. Colonization was a term for theft of property by a bully nation that had bigger guns and boots on the ground.

Like the Americans settling the United States, the ruler authorizes his nation's military to kill native inhabitants so his clan can secure title to the stolen land, so the government can write deeds granting property to the ruler's supporters. The elites simply boast, "We are of a higher class with superior morals and social rules. We're entitled to take what we want from backward savages. If need be, we have the right to kill them."

The English were the most imperialistic, and they felt entitled to every rock. They had to be offensive because they were an island nation. For England to colonize the world, their only choice was to control the seas. They had to have harbors around the world. The English colonized Canada, Australia, India, Africa, New Zealand, and other nations around the globe — and for a while, the United States was an English Colony. By 1900 the imperialistic countries' combined empires covered 85 percent of the world's surface.

In the nineteenth century, Englishman Cecil Rhodes set up a secret society of Anglo intellectuals who allied with the English throne. Their purpose was to start wars and create financial chaos so they could acquire assets and power for England. Rhodes's ultra-conservative group bore the semblance in today's world of an intelligence agency like the CIA. [Y11]

Cecil Rhodes and Lord Randolph Churchill [Winston's father] were close friends of the Rothschilds. Cecil Rhodes, as an agent for the Rothschilds, helped establish De Beers, the diamond monopoly.

Cecil Rhodes was a disciple of John Ruskin who brought concepts like fine arts to Oxford. Rhodes left part of his great fortune to fund the Rhodes Scholarships at Oxford to spread the English ruling class tradition throughout the English-speaking world. [Y12]

Rhodes expressed a belief that his clan was better qualified to run the world because British values could more properly serve mankind. As a supreme optimist, Rhodes stated, "Why should we not form a secret society with but one objective, the furtherance of the British Empire and the bringing of the whole world under British rule, for the recovery of the United States, for making the Anglo-Saxon race but one Empire. What a dream, but yet it is probable; it is possible."

The English developed superior power-schemes. Cecil Rhodes used the concept of imperialism to cause the Boer War for the Empire to gain control of African resources.

Savages were naïve, defenseless people who were going to lose their valuables and possibly their lives. When less civilized tribes with their spears charged the British with fine guns and cannons, they were mowed down. As justification, the Anglo elites espoused the theory that the other groups were inferior people who needed to be civilized.

English newspapers controlled world opinion. The public's opinions had to be swayed to recognize the savages were at fault. The savages were depicted as the aggressor, the group that was responsible for hostility. The savages had to take the blame and pay damages. "Yes, we'll take land, gold, diamonds, whatever you have of value!"

Lawrence James' *Churchill and Empire, a Portrait of an Imperialist* defines the British Empire and the egotist Winston Churchill. Like his father's friend, Cecil Rhodes, Winston believed the British Empire would bring stability and direction to backward natives in return for control of their assets.

Eventually, the English had the land, gold, and diamonds. It was then Winston Churchill recognized the English should abandon their policies of routinely killing thousands of natives on the other side of their Empire, uneducated people who simply opposed colonization. Time to save the ammunition!

The U.S. elite took the same approach as the English. U.S. leaders like Teddy Roosevelt never found a reason to deviate from the English tradition of imperialism. As the U.S. frontier expanded, two new terms were added to the U.S. dictionary – Manifest Destiny and the Monroe Doctrine.

Manifest Destiny meant the U.S. elites were quite superior, and their military was empowered to kill native Indians and take their land.

The Monroe Doctrine was a policy by President James Monroe in 1832 that any intervention by foreign powers in the Americas could be considered a potentially hostile act against the U.S.

Like Abraham Lincoln in the 1800s, Churchill was the man of the century in the 1900s. In 1940, after hard study and making a few big mistakes, Churchill was an aggressive leader who had learned military operations. Past his prime, Churchill was ready to lead when the opportunity arrived. He re-energized and saved England and the United States.

Churchill's mindset was apart from brutal authoritarians like Adolph Hitler and Joseph Stalin. That's why, in his later years, Churchill could become an established writer and an elder statesman.

Hitler's war sought revenge and world power. It was an attempt to establish a German-Italian-Japanese world order, whereas a new Allied group was an attempt by Churchill and Roosevelt to reshuffle the deck with an Anglo-Jewish-French-Saudi-German-Italian-Japanese base. Churchill and Roosevelt locked in more brains, technology, and resources.

The authoritarian desires of the wartime leaders shouldn't be taken negatively. At the time, imperialism was the coin of the realm. Imperialism was a world-order concept where the elites used racism. "That bastard has slant eyes and strange skin. He must be evil. I wish someone would kill him!"

American imperialism began as an extension of English imperialism, and since imperialism is an expression of racism, it inherently survives on a personal level and a national level.

After WW II, John Foster Dulles became the center of military strategy. As a commanding person with unequivocal credentials, he served as the Republican Party foreign affairs spokesman, ran the Just and Durable Peace commission for the Federal Council of Churches, was chairman of the Carnegie Endowment for International Peace, was an elder in the Park Avenue Presbyterian Church, and served as a trustee for both the Rockefeller Foundation and the Union Theological Seminary.

John Foster Dulles' brother Allen was America's super-spy. At the end of WW II, Allen Dulles had the U.S. intelligence, the OSS, recruit Nazi intelligence staffers, and the best German scientists. Allen made Germany's chief intelligence officer, General Reinhart Gehlen, the Allied nation's European intelligence leader. Allen also recruited German rocket scientist Wernher von Braun to be part of the NASA team.

Allen Dulles was appointed as the first director of the CIA. It helped that Allen Dulles was serving as the lawyer for Rockefeller's cabal.

Allen Dulles and John McCloy were a powerful Rockefeller team. McCloy was David Rockefeller's mentor and he helped fund European intelligence. Near the end of their careers, Allen

Dulles and John McCloy served on the Warren Commission before being advisors to President Lyndon Johnson.

The Dulles brothers advocated "Exceptionalism" - the right of the United States to impose their will because the United States knew more, saw further, and lived on a higher moral plane than other nations. [Y13]

Exceptionalism means a nation or a clan believes they are exceptional, and therefore entitled to power. Exceptionalism is an attempt to establish a class distinction to be used as the basis to justify terrorism. Since 2016, the term "Islamic Exceptionalism" has been batted around.

U.S. media never hesitates to remind people how exceptional the U.S. is, but any nation that advocates exceptionalism is racist.

Being racist didn't bother the U.S. public until Donald Trump's election in 2016. The public wasn't taught to distinguish between nationalism and patriotism, but in 2016 the change in the social mix from 10% non-white in 1950 to 34% in 2014 caused white folks to become more racist and shift to the Republican Party. [Y14]

Rule 8: Work hard to understand the big picture. Ignore the political noise, and focus on how you can profit from what is going on while you help society.

War and Oil

General George Washington's army defeated Lord Cornwallis at Yorktown, Virginia because the French fleet under Count de Grasse held off the British fleet.

When Washington was elected as the first President, he set the example of how a President should act. Washington did not try to interfere with Congress or the Supreme Court. As if to tell the public the U.S. would not be a monarchy, Washington did not run for a third term.

Although Washington knew the United States needed the most powerful navy in the world, the concept of a large standing army was contrary to his beliefs. He stated, "Overgrown military establishments are under any form of government inauspicious to liberty, and are to be regarded as particularly hostile to republican liberty."

In a more recent timeframe, John Galbraith's son, James K. Galbraith, wrote about the causes of America's problems. Galbraith's list included the overuse of military power, the rising cost of resources, the digital revolution, and a lack of regulation in the financial sector, all of which led to the "end of normal."

Washington and Galbraith were centuries apart, but the overuse of military power was high on their list of actions contrary to a successful society.

A large standing army jeopardizes financial management and liberty. The burden of an overweight military ultimately squeezes the masses into a corner.

The United States' policy to maintain a huge military was not caused by the Civil War. After the Civil War, the United States was one vast farmland. As in the song America the Beautiful, the Native American's land was a fertile plain surrounded by oceans - a breadbasket from sea to shining sea.

The west was gradually tamed, and rail spanned the continent delivering people and produce. The age of steel and oil brought steel plows and combustion engines. High-horsepower tractors and combines enabled farmers to cover more ground. Irrigation and electrical gins improved crop yields.

Farm sizes increased and work became more specialized, but in 1900, the U.S. industry didn't hinge on crude oil and electricity. Cars and planes were not perfected. The corporate and military worlds were small.

America was making great strides, but England and Europe were still the powers. Before WW I, the English partnered with the international financial capabilities of the Rothschilds because between 1875 and 1916 Germany bypassed Great Britain in every category of production. To reassert itself, the British Empire gambled everything by negotiating secret alliances with Russia and their enemy France. Tsar Romanov agreed Russia would get Constantinople. France would get Alsace-Lorraine, and the Middle East would be carved up. [Y15]

When things were in place, the English created a conflict with Germany. [Y16]

Near the end of WW I, combat ground down to trench warfare. England could not defeat Germany. This stalemate forced England to bring the United States into the conflict.

In 1917, English Foreign Secretary Arthur Balfour issued a declaration for the creation of a Jewish state in Palestine. The British were short on money, and the Balfour Agreement was a carrot to entice Jewish people in the U.S. to help finance the war. The Agreement could influence Americans to have the U.S. enter the war on England's side, and the British hoped the Agreement would secure British control of Palestine and serve as a buffer to Egypt and the Suez Canal.

In a world-order conflict, the media is a dominant weapon. The English blamed WW I on Germany, although it was England who wrote secret agreements with France and Russia, and it was England and France who declared war on Germany.

WW II was caused because the WW I settlement was too biased in favor of France, the nation which suffered the most. The payments to France were onerous, and the German bankers took advantage of the system by inflating the German currency to pay off the debt to France. German money was printed so fast they only bothered to put ink on one side of the paper, causing its value to go from a 1:9 exchange rate with the U.S. dollar in 1919 to utter destruction five years later. [Y17]

When the German currency became worthless, the "Jewish Syndicate" made millions on the devaluation and gained control of Berlin. Better paying jobs went to the Jewish people. The media was entirely in Jewish hands. Non-Jews were squeezed out, and German society broke down with a wave of sexual promiscuity. At the time, less than 5% of the German population was Jewish. As a result, the overt Jewish racism generated a strong anti-Semitic response. [Y18]

This conflict between the Nazis and the Zionists caused German leaders to reach a "Transfer Agreement" to allow the creation of a Jewish Palestine. This agreement allowed 60,000 of the wealthier Jewish residents to buy freedom in exchange for $100M. The agreement saved some lives and rescued certain assets while sacrificing the balance to the fascists.

Hard times enable dictators who would not normally qualify as leaders. If the United States had not entered WW I, England and Germany would likely have fought to a stalemate. If that had occurred, it's quite probable Adolph Hitler would never have risen to power.

The same groups that fought against each other in WW I again fought each other in WW II. The aggressive authoritarianism of Adolph Hitler brought the Great War. Hitler and the German industrial complex sought retaliation against England, France, and Russia.

Hitler began his strategy by recruiting Italy and then the Germany of Asia, Japan.

Adolph Hitler in Germany and Benito Mussolini in Italy rose to power as fascist dictators - nationalistic people who seized power quickly. Like Lenin, Hitler and Mussolini each wrote a book to describe their clan's philosophical superiority.

Crude oil became the most critical resource - required for bigger tanks, faster planes, more powerful ships, and automotive vehicles.

In 1943, a "limitless" quantity of petroleum was discovered under the sands of Arabia. When the first monster well was struck in the 1,000-foot limestone sand, it flowed 100,000 barrels a day through a seven-inch casing.

Franklin Roosevelt stopped in Cairo to meet representatives of Rockefeller's California Standard Oil Company and discuss the significance of the find. Roosevelt immediately ordered the expedited construction of a 50,000-barrel-per-day refinery in Saudi Arabia. [Y19]

The United States climbed into bed with the Saudis. We did a long-term deal; the U.S. would defend and protect the oil fields, and the Saudis would supply the Allied nations with their unlimited oil at a reasonable price.

Rockefeller's California Standard Oil Company was there to participate. Those relationships have endured.

The Saudis have made billions of dollars and worldwide they have invested billions. They have recently been big investors in emerging technology. They realize their oil supplies, similar to what is happening to coal, will be replaced by renewable energy.

The core of the current "Allied" relationship with Saudi Arabia is oil - an ingredient necessary for survival on a global basis. The military can't run without oil, and the Saudis have around 18% of the world's oil reserves. Because of those oil reserves, the death of Jamal Khashoggi did not affect the U.S.-Saudi relationship.

Jared Kushner, son-in-law of Donald Trump, was quick to confirm the Jewish support of Saudi Arabia. That tells you the Saudis are smart and have money and power, and the old treaties are in place. Millions of barrels of oil from Saudi Arabia mean billions of dollars flow into Allied coffers. To the Allied nations, a long-term financial relationship with OPEC is more important than the life of one journalist.

Putin naturally lent support, saying Russian's relationship would remain unchanged - the Saudis can always count on Russia. Screw any journalist who gets in the way!

When Franklin Roosevelt visited the Saudi oil discovery, he was on a trip to a Big Four meeting [Franklin Roosevelt, Winston Churchill, Chiang Kai-shek, and Joseph Stalin]. The leaders were to begin discussing the potential of their victory over the Axis powers.

Churchill and Roosevelt led the U.S. and British think-tanks in laying out a post-war strategy calling for the United States military to dominate the western hemisphere, the Far East, and the former British Empire with its Middle East energy resources. [Y20]

Authors J. Fletcher Prouty and Noam Chomsky referred to the results of those planning sessions respectively as the "Grand Strategy" and the "Grand Area Plans". Those plans meant the U.S. would be the military arm for the Allied nations. England's Royal Navy would be vested in the U.S. Navy. The plans also called for a "new" grouping of Allied nations.

In his 2011 book, *JFK*, Prouty wrote, "The 'Grand Strategy' decision to create a new bi-polar world had already been made in 1944-45, and the partners in this new global power structure were to be the United States, Great Britain, France, Germany, and Japan — three of the WW II victors and two of the vanquished." [Y21]

The strongest Allied powers during WW II were the United States, Great Britain, China, and the Soviet Union, but the Grand Area plans left China and the Soviet Union out of the new alliance.

To make the Allied group have a solid purpose, the planners created the strategy for the Cold War or the "Iron

Curtain." Churchill and Roosevelt created a conflict so the military would have a cause. The Allied nations needed an adversary.

Churchill may have distrusted Russia because during WW I Lenin backed out of their agreement to fight Germany. Lenin made the right decision. A large number of the Russian military threw their weapons down and went AWOL. They were disenchanted with war, ripe to join Lenin's revolution.

The United States and England used the adversarial concept because they understood the principles of elitism. For a group or a nation to take a strong position on an issue, it helps to have an adversary who takes the opposite position. This relationship needs to be built up in the press.

The struggle against Nazism had to be replaced when Hitler was defeated. Russia became the designated adversary. Communism was made to sound worse than Nazism and the "Communist" threat was the argument for maintaining a superior military.

J. Edgar Hoover had the big picture. He placed four hundred FBI agents in New York to investigate communists, and four agents to track the La Costa Nostra, the Italian Mafia. [Y22] Murder Incorporated was not on Hoover's list because communism was the anointed adversary.

Communism was a convenient excuse used by racists. Hoover's friend, H.L. Hunt, said he hated Jews and Martin Luther King because they helped spread communism.

The same reasoning was used by Evangelicals when they defended Donald Trump's withholding foreign aid to Ukraine under the premise that the Ukrainian government needed to investigate the Bidens. The Evangelicals used communism as justification for Trump's alleged bribery, saying, "When you are dealing with Marxists, what are you supposed to do? Just take it?" That was typical West Texas mentality, especially around Lubbock.

To build on one-world plans, Japan and Germany were brought into the Allied group so Russia could be isolated. The Allied nations chosen to align were creative and thoughtful. These people had strong work ethics. The nations had the potential to operate as democracies with intellectual liberty.

During planning sessions, Churchill and Roosevelt had heated exchanges on the subject of "the end of colonialism in Southeast Asia." Plans were made for continued warfare in Indochina, Korea, and Indonesia. [Y23] The plans called for medium-sized wars every 15 years.

Half of the U.S. military weapons left in stock at the end of WW II were shipped to Korea and the other half to Indochina, which includes Cambodia and Vietnam. The first war began in Korea in 1950. The next war began in Vietnam in 1965. [Y24]

In an attempt to isolate the enemy in Korea and Vietnam, the Allied forces lost a total of over 100,000 troops. Those losses strained the public's patience to support military conflicts. Losing wars leaves dissension.

Wars don't have to be big wars. They can be like the Iraq War, followed by the ISIS conflict in Syria. To keep the American public dialed in, the wars needed to be smaller and take place on the other side of the globe, away from home. It's easier to control the media if the war isn't next door.

Theories of Society and War, by Klaus Schlichte in 2007, was a study of wars. It concluded the world has more wars, 90% occur in third world countries, wars last longer, and wars have decreased in major nations.

John Foster Dulles was President Eisenhower's most prominent advisor. As the epitome of conservatism, Dulles spewed war in a period when our war machine believed "war provides a sense of external necessity without which no government can long remain in power." [Y25]

Is it possible the Allied nations encouraged the outbreak of hostilities in Korea and Vietnam? They may have hoped smaller wars would help avoid the domino effect, in which case they didn't mind causing a domino effect.

History shows the U.S. elites have a policy of causing wars to control other nations. They hope to profit from oil and other resources. This keeps the younger generation busy and culls a few people.

The think-tanks, like the CFR and Iron Mountain, were proficient at analyzing the advantages of war. Their conclusions never became public, but they were used to formulate military policy.

In 1941, the CFR originally defined the term "Grand Area" as a landmass the U.S. would want to control and defend if the U.S. got into a war with Germany and Japan. At the time, Germany controlled Europe and Japan dominated their region.

The definition of the Grand Area became specific when Churchill and Roosevelt had their military planners create the secret "Grand Area" plans. The discovery of a limitless supply of oil in Saudi Arabia caused the Allies to focus more on protecting Saudi Arabia. Also, including Germany and Japan in the new group caused the structure of the Grand Area to evolve.

The CFR was the first to use the term "domino theory." Their analysis influenced the Grand Area plans to have a small war every 15 years. The Allied nations tried to neutralize the ability of their enemies to start other countries to fail.

The concept of NATO also originated from CFR discussion groups, but again it was the WW II military plans that made things happen. NATO was the Allied Nations' front. NATO would be set up in London. In 1952 it was moved to Paris. In 1967 it was moved to Brussels.

Wars have made the U.S. what it is. The Pentagon became a center of power as the industrial complex became the lab for weapons technology. The U.S. military tested new planes, tanks, and ships.

The CFR was a source of information that allowed members of the elite to profit from wars. The Anglo-Israeli elites used the CFR to influence foreign affairs. [Y26]

The CFR member list included the Dulles family, the CEOs of oil and technology companies, the Rockefellers, top military and intelligence people, and other prominent members of the establishment. For example, the CEOs of Rockefeller's Standard Oil, Humble Oil, and Shell were CFR members.

The home base of the CFR has been New York, the home town of the Roosevelts and the Rockefellers.

At the end of WW II, the Japanese air force didn't have enough fuel to send planes up to defend Japan. The atomic bombs were unnecessary. Japanese defeat was assured, but the thought of defeat was a black swan to the Japanese. They were preparing to fight to the last soldier.

Harry Truman had the atomic bombs dropped because he didn't want to waste Allied lives. The Allied army had to visually prove they had the ultimate weapon to prevent losing more lives.

War is like football, chess, and poker. The goal is victory, and to rule over others. The elites want to control and to avoid catastrophic conflict. They concentrate on making all the money. They have learned to sit and wait for the vision of the black swan to appear to everyone.

Post-WW II plans called for the U.S. military to represent a new Allied group of nations. The U.S. Navy would defend Saudi Arabia's oil supplies and support the Allied nations like the Royal Navy previously defended the British Colonies.

Churchill and Roosevelt isolated Russia as their adversary to make the Allied one-world game consequential. The Grand Area plans allowed the British Empire and U.S. oligarchs to pursue their one-world strategy and profit from the wars.

David Rockefeller's cabal of one-world advocates used NATO, the FED, the CFR, and corporations to control other nations and profitably finance wars. The Grand Area plans encouraged the Korean and Vietnam wars to avoid the potential of a "domino effect", which might be caused by an adversary, like Russia.

That story was never offered to the sheep. This Cold War environment was created to keep the public involved in the game that made the Russians our terrible enemy. Churchill and Roosevelt set that scenario up at the end of WW II so elites like the Rockefellers could take advantage of their position. They used the religious lie and mafias to retain position.

In 1956, *The Power Elites* by C. Wright Mills chronicled the evolution of the new military-corporate elites. Mills' book examined how the white-collar corporate elites and the military establishment became the voice of America as power shifted from the rural countryside and corporate boardrooms to the military-industrial complex, as Dwight D. Eisenhower referred to it.

Mills' book failed to mention the Grand Area strategy. Pre-2010 history also seems to be silent on the plans for the U.S. to dominate the Grand Area. Those plans were classified. Few people had access - only members of the CFR, top military staff, government leaders, and oligarchs.

Rule 9: A person needs to understand the past so he or she can navigate through the maze and contribute. An individual can't afford to get crosswise with the elites; he or she must appear to be neutral. To have substance, be part of a movement to improve the future of the world.

Power

We owe it to ourselves, and to each other, to understand the world as it appears before us, not as we might remember it or hope it will be again. [Y27] Ohio Republican Senator John Kasich.

To make decisions for your future, a person needs to understand world power and the role of Allied oligarchs.

In 1900, the English were ahead of everyone in planning. Being an island-nation clan with colonies, the English looked beyond the continent-based masses.

England and France used their influence to drag the U.S into WW I; otherwise, there would have been a stalemate. The same nations fought in WW II, and the Jewish-WASP elites in England again used their influence to bring the United States into a conflict where the Catholics were caught in the middle.

At the end of WW II, the world was forced down a conflicted path when the CFR's Grand Area plans were used as the strategy to initiate limited wars every 15 years. The purpose of wars was to eliminate the possibility of a domino effect initiated by competitive nations.

Churchill and Roosevelt created a world order. The world-order game allowed elites to enjoy worldly perks. The elites didn't care how long the game persisted. They assumed their class system and wealth would prevail. The elites used enormous sums of taxpayer money to influence politicians and media spokesmen. Their power turned followers into facilitators.

The one-world mentality became clearer in 1976 when additional plans were advocated by Henry Kissinger. In *The Rockefeller File* by Gary Allen, syndicated columnist Paul Scott explained the enhanced strategy: "By controlling food, one can control people, and by controlling energy, especially oil, one can control nations and their financial systems. By placing food and oil under international control along with the world's monetary system, [Henry] Kissinger is convinced a loosely knit world government can become reality by 1980."

Kissinger worked for the Rockefellers - the wealthy New York family controlling the FED and the oil industry. Kissinger believed the Allied group needed to focus on controlling food in addition to oil. He insinuated the groups' monetary system could facilitate this process - presumably the FED, the International Monetary Fund [IMF], and the World Bank [WB]. The IMF and WB were set up in 1940 by the CFR. The oligarchs' plans must have been to control nations.

Kissinger postulated the Allied nations would be able to finish creating their world order by 1980. Kissinger extended the Grand Area plans, but he was a four decades off. What Kissinger missed was that the Catholics would have to reconnect with the Jewish Syndicate in order to gain control of the U.S. political system, and it would take a two decades to destroy the fundamental Muslims in the Middle East. Those issues have been resolved except for Iran.

As Kissinger's corollary spread, the Allied elites began working more diligently to create their invasive species - one group of ethnically different nations secretly using the Allied military and huge financial resources to control the world.

That may have been about the time seed-companies began developing products that would only be good for one year, where farmers would have to buy new seeds every year.

In 1980, Alvin Toffler published *The Third Wave*. The first wave was an agricultural wave which had small communities living off the land. The second wave was an industrial revolution where the masses moved to larger cities and took jobs.

At the time, Toffler saw an exciting, innovative future, but he did not foresee the rise of digital software and the advancement of China. Toffler didn't visualize microprocessors, cell-phones, the Internet, and artificial intelligence. Neither did anyone else.

If you examine the index of *The Third Wave* and follow all the China references, Toffler missed the rise of China. China was not moving forward in 1980. China had millions of people and rice paddies. Richard Nixon brought together the Chinese leaders, those with vision. Since then, China has done more in 20 years than the U.S. did in 60 years.

Toffler's *Third Wave* proved it's impossible to project more than two decades ahead. No one can foresee the next major innovations, war, or depression. Who seems brilliant at a moment will be gone with the wind in the future. All one can do is offer shorter-term analysis. This is also true in the financial markets where the window to the future is shorter, perhaps a mere few weeks.

China succeeded because they were not politically bound up. They embraced technology and were not encumbered with trying to maintain a one-world society. They did have huge problems, like too many people.

If you thought Trump was blunt, ask the Tibetans about China. The Chinese brought in the highest 2% of their scholars and pursued doing the big things correctly. They created an intellectual democracy and monarchy. They had seen what happened to the Japanese, and they didn't let the Allied nations trap them.

The elites support politicians and they expect tax breaks. As Donald Trump's term began, his administration reduced the elites' taxes and increased the military's budget. Trump's agenda was destined to run trillion dollar deficits. Reagan's presidency proved those actions yield big negative numbers.

The potential deficits were ignored by Republicans. Trump's focus was to help his donors and began installing the oligarch's new plan, the concept of a new world order. His administration began working on restructuring trade agreements with other nations.

The border wall and the impeachment process served as noise to obscure the trade negotiations. The elite's game used racism and the GOP had no qualms of destroying democracy if they can gain total control. They tried to enlist the military to take over.

The conservative sheep always fall for the elites' story. This last play probably began a decade before Donald Trump was elected President. In 2016, the elites started the conflict with the border wall promise. Trump immediately ran into opposition. Hordes of aliens possible paid for by Soros, or some oligarch, took buses to the border as Trump struggled to get a wall built. The wall and the hordes of aliens were planned. It did not happen spontaneously. The same for the fires. Australia was a test. We are looking at massive treason, and only people who could do this are some fascists in the Pentagon who are egged on to run the world.

In early 2018, Xi Jinping and his ranking military leaders met Donald Trump at Trump's mansion in Palm Beach. They relaxed and discussed a mutual agenda for North Korea. Those oligarchs would never have met that casually if the plans to do so weren't developed years earlier. There are just too many layers of Deep State management for anything to happen quickly.

Then, in April 2018, Song Tao, head of the Chinese Communist International Department, visited North Korean leader Kim Jong Un to discuss the future of China and North Korea. Shortly thereafter, North Korea and South Korea meet and set bold goals – peace and no nuclear weapons.

In June, President Trump met with Kim Jong Un to hammer out a minimal overview of a potential deal. Afterward, Kim Jong Un met with Chinese President Xi Jinping at the ornate Great Hall of the People in the Chinese Capitol. Then in July, Trump and Putin meet to discuss the issues.

Although it might seem unrelated, in September, the Catholic Church agreed to a pastoral agreement with China to allow the Chinese to appoint Chinese Bishops. This was similar to the deal Napoleon Bonaparte cut centuries earlier where he got to appoint the French Bishops.

The Catholics are tremendously powerful. They have billions of followers across the planet. They have multiple supporters on the Supreme Court; the Pope can wear red shoes and weird robes, and he can dismiss Mike Pompeo.

In October 2018, Trump espoused nationalism and French President Macron defined nationalism as the opposite of patriotism. Macron followed up by saying France was not the U.S.'s vassal - a script that took some sharp French writers.

In early 2019, Warren Buffett and his partner Charlie Munger joined the circus when they pandered to the Chinese during their company's annual shareholder's meeting. They offered their "I love you China" chip. "I can't wait to invest in Chinese companies."

A few months later, Henry Kissinger hobbled over to meet Xi to reinforce the new U.S.-China relationship. He said:

"It is no longer possible to think that one side can dominate the other. So, those countries that used to be exceptional and used to be unique, have to get used to the fact that they have a rival. … Competition is permanent."

The elites' pawns could work together for financial and social balance, but that's not normally the way the game is played. Working together could end the elites' gravy train. They would lose their swagger and have to work again.

After WW II, Allied leaders could have used technocrats to re-engineer society, but the oligarchs believed they were entitled and control was just a matter of developing tight legal and social networks to give themselves an edge. To share, the elites would have had to think outside the box. Instead, they chose to create static social structures to reduce risk as they increased their grip on the public.

The world no longer needs more manufacturing capability to have a good life. The world needs fewer people, fewer politics, and a smaller military.

The United States and China are pretending to have an unfriendly relationship. The oligarchs hope to generate nationalism and polarize their sheep. This adversarial game normally works because the public gets caught up in chaos.

The elites' pawns must feel important and in control. They aren't secure or intelligent enough to share power. That's part of why the English ambassador to the U.S. described Trump as insecure and incompetent. Trump was!

The super-power elites can't have their pawns consummating deals. Americans can't trust the Chinese or the Russians, and vice-versa. Sharing would destroy the game. The elites must be able to parade around and enjoy the perks. Everything is a big lie.

In the past, the Democrats were too ill-prepared to complain when Reagan ran with a trickle-down agenda. Times were good. There was a strong middle-class and no one could clearly prove trickle-down wouldn't work.

Around 2000, GOP leaders, led by George W. Bush and Haliburton, began to privatize social security, Medicare, the post office, the military, and any government function that would make money for investors. The masses were not given any opportunity to participate.

The public needed a George W. Bush followed by a docile Barack Obama followed by an authoritarian to visualize why voting is so important. Trump went to the extreme. He thought he could do what he wanted, whether Congress approved or not.

If public leaders would restructure the government and made sure workers were properly grandfathered, instead of the President writing executive orders so a friend and donor of his could take over the business, then it might be fine to alter what has worked for decades.

In the decades before Newt Gingrich initiated an adversarial relationship between the two parties, Congress had more moderate and honorable politicians. Sometimes Congressmen worked together before they fell into the trap of looting the Treasury.

The GOP has the resources to orchestrate any type of world-order play. Just throw another trillion on the table.

The masses aren't stupid, but they are too busy and subconsciously they have no power. Voters are polarized to the extent that the only strength they feel is when they discuss politics with their biased peers.

The masses have been taught that the elites are like God, invisible. This concept allows elites to run the United States without criticism. An author writes about the elites is ostracized - described as racist or worse. Even publishing a book about the conflict between elites and technology is a violation of protocol.

Our increasingly digital society allowed open-minded technocrats from China to understand how the elites function, but the bulk of the U.S. public is not intelligent enough to see the *reset* play. The masses are caught up by media noise and politicians confuse the public as this white, racist skit evolves.

Now, because of the Internet, voters are beginning to grasp the damage the elites have caused. The public has begun to resist the cavalier attitude of oligarchs. In October of 2019, the Democratic presidential candidates' voices all cried, "Tax the rich."

The public used to question if a big monetary gift was bribery, but now big gifts are ignored. The Republicans couldn't bring themselves to even politely criticize Trump's acceptance of casino funds and racism.

There was a reason Sheldon Adelson gave Donald Trump a $25M political donation shortly before the 2016 election, just as there was a reason for the DOJ to rule online gambling was illegal in early 2019.

The United States has an opportunity to end this intrigue. Neither 100% socialism nor 100% capitalism works. Voters need to energize around a practical plan. A new administration needs to empower intellectuals and technocrats to draft new rules with a flexible social platform to allow the sheep to participate.

Americans should not allow the elite media games to obscure what should be done. The public needs to discuss creating a fair social system for the masses before 5G and artificial intelligence decimates our society. The elites need to be made more transparent! The world doesn't need powerful puppeteers. Elites can be easily retrained and refocused. China proved that.

H.L. Mencken was right. Democracy protects the man who is inferior, regiments men by force, makes them as much alike as possible and destroys originality.

Democracy allows the Allied elites to use rigged systems to rob from the poor. The elites defined a financial system through the use of their international banks and fiat money to build a social structure to control the governments of the world.

The elites started by giving themselves an edge, and until now an individual couldn't circumvent the elites' system. But, with digital technology changing the world, the Deep State and religion are dispensable, assuming the masses have a voice. The Pope and the Queen are dispensable if there is a real plan for rational order.

The Allied elites want to keep their sheep penned. If voters understood, they could energize around a practical agenda for a fairer social system. Intellectuals and technocrats could draft new rules for a more enjoyable planet. The problem is that most people don't understand technology and have to go along with their peers. It's impossible for the sheep to visualize how to replace the oligarch's hierarchical system.

The masses intuitively realize they aren't ready to dispense with the leadership. Change is a question of understanding, and it is certainly the time to analyze the NWO and our dysfunctional social structures. The new digital-age window will only continue to unfold, and that opportunity will enlarge.

Rule 10: Seek power by associating with those who have power. Relax and learn to use the system. Listen to Etta Jane's *At Last*, kick back, and think about it. Work to give the masses a voice in real issues.

Conspiracies

At the end of WW I, the Allied nations tried to set up a League of Nations, which would have been comparable to NATO. That didn't succeed. Instead, WW I led to WW II.

Since WW II, people have been trapped by the one-world media controlled by Allied oligarchs. The public has been influenced to ignore conspiracies, and once the media lies, they stay committed. The masses have not been given real facts. The government and the media couldn't afford to tell the masses what was going on because the masses would have been upset.

Even though the oligarchs have the all-power CIA as their front, things are changing. The conspiracies are becoming fact. The conspiracy of Pearl Harbor, the assassinations of the 1960s, the 9-11 false flag, and even the Trump presidency are easily explained. A few key elements define the conspiracies. Any unsolved conspiracies can be deduced, solved by asking subject matter experts [SMEs], or by merely considering who wound up with the money and power.

All major conspiracies were proven by the summer of 2020. Lew Rockwell published reports with accurate evidence verifying Pearl Harbor was an anticipated event. Interestingly, an informed person would have had an overview of the Pearl Harbor conspiracy if he read A. Ralph Epperson *The Unseen Hand*, which was published in 1985. Epperson solved the Pearl Harbor story, but it took decades for the media to flesh out FDR's lies.

Mainstream media never admitted they covered up the Pearl Harbor attack. Pearl Harbor was simple: 1) The U.S. Navy removes its carriers to Wake and Midway and leaves older ships. 2) Before Pearl Harbor, the Europeans break the German code which the Japanese fleet is using. 3) The Japanese fleet leaves after the attack instead of returning the next day because they realize no carriers were sunk. 4) The U.S. fleet miraculously knew exactly where the Japanese fleet was at Midway!

Conspiracy nuts are sheep who deny conspiracies. The expression *Lone Nutter* means a person is a stupid sheep who believes Lee Harvey Oswald killed President Kennedy. Don't be a Lone Nutter. The JFK assassination was solved many times.

In the 2019-2020 time span, Ron Paul, who was regularly seen with Lew Rockwell, offered a video where he described the JFK assassination as a conspiracy with the CIA at the core. 1) The master project-leader for military assassinations, CIA General Edward Lansdale, was at the Dealey Plaza. Previously, Lansdale reported to Allen Dulles. 2) Bethesda, a CIA-Navy managed facility, was used for the falsified autopsy. 3) Prominent people like Lodge and Johnson whispered to their friends, "It was the CIA."

In 1973, casually, CIA Director [DCIA] William Colby verified the CIA's control of all major U.S. media sources. Allen Dulles, J. Edgar Hoover, and Lyndon Johnson contained the media and pressured the television networks to endorse the lone assassin theory.

When Oliver Stone produced his *JFK* movie, the critics, supporters of the conspirators, picked out a few discrepancies and enlarged them. People like Lyndon Johnson's man in Hollywood, Jack Valenti, were all over Stone for suggesting there was a conspiracy.

Lyndon Johnson was a tremendous domestic administrator and an enormous schemer. Johnson had Jack Valenti "promoted" to be president of the Academy of Motion Picture Arts and Sciences. One of Johnson's Jewish sponsors, Lew Wasserman, met weekly with Valenti and other AMPAS lawyers and producers. For four decades, Valenti and the titans of the movie industry protected Johnson.

With the threat of murder, the publishers would not take on the other media outlets, the President, and the directors of the FBI and CIA. The media convicted Lee Harvey Oswald without a trial. Despite hundreds of pieces of evidence, the media didn't present the truth. Dozens of witnesses were killed. This allowed the lone assassin theory to become fact for many adults.

My last book also has an excellent chapter on the JFK assassination. My friend Robert P. Morrow was the SME on that chapter.

I asked someone about producing a series on all the conspiracies up to the Washington coup. He summed up the situation: "Since Stone's JFK came out, Hollywood has such a powerful CIA control that none of these types of films can be made in mainstream studios. Several were underway and apparently were blocked by 'hidden forces.' Don't want to discourage you, but several friends have worked years on getting films made and a few had major studio contracts but they were all stopped without explanation."

Another writer and movie producer commented, "I talked to the military records at the Pentagon a few years past, asking if I could get copies of some of my Naval Intelligence investigations and/or MLK/JFK assassination investigation records, related to some of my intelligence work. He said, 'Those records are in a box in a warehouse where even those responsible to protect them know nothing about them. You can be sure no one will ever see them.'"

"All we can do is try to connect the dots based on what we personally know. There are still some details I avoid or just don't talk about. I have exhausted my investigations, as far as finding new or other real evidence, all else has been destroyed or is in a Top Secret classification or Above Top Secret, so it's gone or will never be seen."

The 9-11 conspiracy also was never complex. After the attack, I heard from a Jewish person in Santa Fe that Jewish employees in the WTC were told not to show up at work on 9-11. About a week after the WTC attack, a Beirut television station reported that 4,000 Israeli employees were absent the day of the attack.

The Jewish Syndicate and the CIA were aware in advance of the pending attack. There are many well written chapters on this subject.

In March 2020, an investigation by the University of Alaska Fairbanks verified the collapse of Building 7 in the World Trade Center was caused by controlled demolition. Dan Rather may have been the first to speculate if building 7 came down because of controlled demolition.

U.S. government reports concluded the collapse was the result of a fire. Building 7 was supposedly the tallest building to ever collapse because of a fire.

One does not take a 47 story building down with a controlled demolition unless it is planned. Associates of Rupert Murdock leased Building 7 for $100,000 six weeks before the WTC attack. After the WTC attack, they sued an insurance company for $7 billion.

A group of Israeli intelligence men filmed the planes flying into both WTC buildings. They were picked up by the FBI and several weeks later they were released and they flew back to Israel.

The Zionists took advantage of their position. 9-11 was allowed because it would propel the U.S. into a Middle East War. Israeli intelligence and the CIA coordinated with the White House.

On May 12, 2020, the FBI inadvertently also tied the Saudis to the WTC attack. For those who reviewed the George W. Bush and Saudi Prince Bandar relationship, that wasn't a surprise. 9-11 was a false-flag operation and it follows that the intelligence community, the Jewish Syndicate, the mafias, the FBI, and both political parties will never allow anyone to investigate the WTC attack because the threads run back to the oligarchs.

The Zionists and the CIA were not investigated because "federal" law enforcement was controlled by President George W. Bush and he was not about to go against the oligarchs. He comes from a family that was closely aligned with the Rockefellers.

There has been enormous pressure to break this story, but the WTC crime could not be investigated while Trump was in office. Trump also had Jewish connections.

The false-flag operation of 9-11 was obvious. The Jewish Syndicate had enough media control to maintain a lie, but they shouldn't have told Jewish workers to stay home on 9-11. The WTC attack was a disgrace, but being pragmatic and arrogant, the Israelis believe they can deny their deplorable act.

The Liberty ship attack was another lie - the result of Lyndon Johnson's connection to the Israeli elites. Johnson's connections trace back to his political connection to Senator Kleberg, a Jewish Senator from Texas who had ownership in the King Ranch. Johnson also used Jewish lawyers like Abe Fortas to help his rise to the Senate. Johnson's ties to the Jewish film industry helped him contain the JFK evidence.

I also reviewed Lyndon Johnson's and Richard Nixon's theft of billions of dollars worth of gold. This is a story that has never been distributed because of the elite's power.

On Saturday, July 25, 2020, I drove to Las Cruces, New Mexico to meet with a historian who writes as John Clarence. John Clarence is the co-author of *The Gold House*. *The Gold House* describes how in 1937 Doc Noss and his wife Ova Noss discovered a tremendous cache of partially smelted Spanish gold bricks in caves at Victorio Peak. There were billions of dollars worth of 60% gold bricks stored in caves near Las Cruses.

Doc Noss took on Charley Ryan as a partner and Ryan shot and killed Noss in an argument near the Victorio Peak gold mines. Eventually, the military at White Sands found out about the gold and *illegally* confiscated Ova Noss's property by annexing it as part of the White Sands military base. Then military officials began stealing the Victorio Peak treasure.

When the military's theft of Doc Noss's treasure came to the attention of President Jack Kennedy, he began a process of resolving this issue. Just before he was assassinated, he was trying to schedule a meeting to compensate Mrs. Noss with a share of the gold.

After Kennedy was assassinated, Lyndon Johnson initially took no action on the gold. Then, near the end of his term, when Johnson realized he had no chance of winning re-election, Johnson bought a 100,000-acre ranch in Mexico that had an airstrip. Before Johnson left the presidency, he had a military pilot airlift billions of dollars worth of gold to his Mexico ranch. Johnson stored the gold bars at the ranch in Mexico because FDR had made it illegal for a U.S. citizen to own gold. The stolen gold was later smelted in Canada and the profits were deposited to Johnson's accounts.

Johnson didn't take all of the gold, and Richard Nixon was Lyndon Johnson's protégé and backup. Historian John Clarence has documentation that the military, Richard Nixon, and banking officials worked to steal as much gold *legally* as they could.

Nixon had a law passed making it legal for an American citizen to own gold. When Nixon was about to be removed from office, he had thirty-seven tons of gold transported to a California storage facility over Thanksgiving weekend in 1973. Nixon had the gold smelted and sold so his share of the profits could be deposited to his bank account. [These events were also written up in Roger Stone's bestseller, *The Man Who Killed Kennedy.* beginning on page 410.]

Johnson and Nixon stayed within the law on the possession of gold. A Franklin Roosevelt, Dwight Eisenhower, John Kennedy, or a Jimmy Carter probably would never have stolen the gold. The Democrat Johnson and the Republican Nixon stole all they could, but the Democrat Kennedy didn't and he tried to fairly compensate Mrs. Noss.

The important things related to this story are: First, honesty is individual. Therefore, vetting the candidates is required to restore any honor to the system. The public needs to question each candidate. A television session where people verbally stab each other and answer selected questions is inadequate. A lie-detector test should be included. Forget looking presidential! Eliminate the scumbags. Ask real personal questions!

Second, the participants are always the politicians, the military leaders, the bankers, and the lawyers. Those groups are necessary to move and legally transfer the money. Once the president makes solid connections with the military and financial authorities, the president can do just about anything.

On January 19, 2019, Martin Luther King Jr. Day, a group of prominent citizens petitioned Congress to reopen the investigations of the assassinations of President John F. Kennedy, Malcolm X, Martin Luther King Jr., and Senator Robert F. Kennedy.

The petitioning group included Kennedy and King family members, doctors, a coroner, celebrities, and others. They are The Truth & Reconciliation Committee on the Assassinations of the 1960s. This group is headed by David Talbot, a distinguished writer – slightly knowledgeable on the Kennedys, Allen Dulles, and the CIA. Oliver Stone was also a member of the petition group.

The U.S. Records Act called for the release of relevant documents in 2017. President Trump defied the U.S. Records Act. Trump had to because the CIA is the 800-pound gorilla. The CIA strongly influenced the presidential campaign. In 2016 and 2020, intelligence people actively supported Donald Trump on social media. As a possible reward to the CIA and mafias for their support, Trump approved an executive order to suppress the release of JFK information.

The petition committee was designed to correct history. They consisted of rich and/or famous people who for the most part believed the United States needed to put the past assassinations in place as history so this country could move forward and discuss real issues.

The committee may issue a report their findings in the spring of 2021. I anticipate several writers would publish books on this subject after the committee releases its report. Talbot's group should have been able to document Johnson, Hoover, the CIA, and the Mafia as conspirators.

The large number of sixty people and the injection of many rich and famous people who were not subject matter experts will add confusion. Any committee of sixty people has to include a few who are biased.

This committee has a Rockefeller and numerous Jewish consultants on it. The Rockefellers were the richest family in the U.S. They controlled the FED and the oil refining industry. No Rockefeller should have been on this committee. Nelson Rockefeller became Vice President, but he wanted to be president. He should have been a prime suspect.

Nelson's brother David gave $100M to Harvard, a good Jewish institution for lawyers. David was like a point guard dealing with powerful political leaders. David and Nelson were a team for years.

The best JFK Subject Matter Experts were not on the assassinations committee. This committee had too many Jews on it. This action had to be a cold deck - a stacked deck that is secretly inserted in the game.

Many of the petition group were sincere. They were brought in to make the committee look legitimate, but experts could put together a handful of people who could produce answers in a month. This is a typical cover-up!

Eisenhower saw it coming: "In the councils of government, we must guard against the acquisition of unwarranted influence, whether sought or unsought, by the military-industrial complex. The potential for the disastrous rise of misplaced power exists, and will persist."

The money spent on politics and the military has enlarged the elites' control. One can only wonder what Eisenhower's views would be now. Eisenhower was Jewish, and like FDR, he didn't need to lie.

The victim families need to see the conspirators on trial, but who would launch such trials? After Hoover passed on, the FBI fell under the control of the CIA and DOJ. There is little likelihood the Jewish Syndicate and the CIA can ever be investigated. They are essentially powerful mafias. You would have to replace too many of them.

Several debate groups attribute the JFK assassination to analogies that go back centuries; in many cases, the obvious Washington political connections are ignored.

Extract yourself from crazy theories and use experts to solve the simple conspiracies so you can move on. A few SMEs, like Phillip Nelson and Robert P. Morrow, speak the truth of the conspiracies and of LBJ.

Rule 11: Congress needs to pass legislation granting amnesty so we can move past the assassinations of the 1960s, but the oligarchs have corrupted the media to fragment and confuse public opinion. Read and seek the truth about conspiracies. Synthesize what's offered and move on.

The CIA capitalizes on rigged elections. Robert Kennedy was wrong about some things, but his assessment that the CIA was worse than the mafias was correct.

Robert Kennedy was a SME on the mafias because his father, Joe Kennedy, was part of the Irish mafia. Since Joe's bootlegging days, the mafias controlled many larger cities, especially in Northern states. Boston, New York, and Chicago were and still are run by the mafias.

Joe Kennedy was Jack's manager. Joe had the money and connections. Joe's being Irish mafia didn't surface as a debate issue when Jack ran for president.

Joe's undisclosed past allowed him to buy the Illinois vote by using the Italian Mafia. In the winter of 1959-1960, Joe flew to Chicago to negotiate for the support of Mafia chief Sam Giancana in the office of William J. Tuohy, a chief justice in Cook County and Joe's old friend. [Y28]

In the early morning hours, the day after the election, the popular vote was too close to call. Oscar Wyatt sat in his plane on a Corpus Christi runway all night with $100,000 in cash. He was prepared to fly to Mississippi to buy their 10 Electoral College delegates.

Wyatt's plane never left the ground because Illinois came in with 27 electoral votes for Jack Kennedy. That gave Jack a comfortable 300 to 219 margin, although he only led the popular vote by a .3% margin. [Y29]

If Joe hadn't bought the Illinois vote, Jack would have lost. Similar types of manipulation go on today. Major elections are *always* rigged, and they are getting more sophisticated.

After the Jack Kennedy assassination, the CIA realized there were easier ways to control the elections. The JFK assassination also strengthened the CIA because it tightly bonded them to the Mafia and the Jewish Syndicate. It forced the CIA to devote enormous resources to influencing the elections because Congressional support was critical to their goals. They realized that if a group can control the President then it can control the military and the DOJ.

I had a close friend who had taught at the Naval War College. He frequented the Pentagon every summer for a month. He said to me, "Bob, do you remember when Senator Sam Nunn retired? Do you remember that three or four times as many than normal Congressmen retired that year?"

I did, and I replied, "Yes, and that seemed strange."

My friend continued, "Well, some of the retired CIA boys found that a lot of politicians were stealing government money and dumping it into Swiss bank accounts, so they confiscated the money and left a note for the crooks: 'You can retire or we will go public with the stolen money.'"

That did not leave any room for the crooked Congressmen to manipulate. Both the house and senate flipped from Democrat to Republican. Here are the mid-term numbers that crushed Clinton's administration:

		House		Senate	
Congress	Term	Dem	Rep	Dem	Rep
103rd	93-94	258	176	57	43
104th	95-96	204	230	48	52
		—	—	—	—
		-54	+54	-9	+9

Newt Gingrich took credit for Republican's mid-term victory, but it was the CIA purge that caused a reversal of fortunes for the Republican Party. I have written this up a couple of times, but the media won't print the truth because they get their perks from the oligarchs.

The 2020 election was the most apparent attempt at a rigged election of all time. In the beginning, Donald Trump wanted to make a couple hundred million more. He did! The oligarchs hung the cheese out there so they could make a couple trillion the easy way.

Placating Pence wasn't complicated. Pence had little money to speak of. He could barely afford an expensive inaugural gown for his wife. Now, Pence's understanding of campaign money has changed under Trump's tutelage. In politics, if your problem is money, you don't have a problem.

Here was the plot as it was explained to me several months before the election: Groups like QAnon were to created chaos and pull polarized supporters into their web. Trump was going to lose to Biden by a small vote. A complaint would go to SCOTUS and they were going to rule Trump was the winner. That would upset the Democrats. The Republican groups would then pull together the rabid Democrats and cause them to start a riot. When that started, the conservatives would come in and crush them in a real coup. The conservative white boys would take over, "like they did in Russia".

That was the background script I heard maybe seven months before the election. I neither understood it or thought it was possible, but when the riot in Washington occurred on January 6, 2021, I knew the plans were real. And, if I heard of the coup ahead of time, that meant a lot of people had to know. Give me a break! I have very few connections.

I did get a partial confirmation of this plan in early October, and I sent a text about it to a friend who handles investments on October 8, 2020:

Well, a Saudi guy came into Houston and he purchased more storage space for oil than is in the Strategic Reserve. This was about 3 weeks ago. When asked who would win the Presidency, he thought Biden would win and get overruled by a Supreme Court judge because of voter fraud.

I called a big GOP guy about this and he said Biden was a 70 30 favorite, and if he was dead, he would still win; there would be no judicial review.

I will not vote. Because I'm writing a book, I want to try to remain impartial. [I found that was impossible, but I was able to more easily do research with that premise.]

Trump has made mistake after mistake. That's why the vote will be strongly against him. Trump also has incompetent campaign managers; he just won't shut up. That is the reality I see.

My friend's reply was:

Some of mistakes are spun to look that way; some are just the result of his ego. Don't fall victim to fake news. They missed the call 4 years ago, remember?

If you are Joe PickupTruck, in the voting booth and you think: What if Biden does [win], which isn't out of the question, this obnoxious negro Kamala Harris will be leading our country against formidable foes, like Putin, the canny Chinese, N. Korea, etc. and what would she do with all the immigration statues that are in place?

It's going to be interesting as hell this election. I don't vote either. Never have because I don't want to do jury duty; I'm selfish with my time.

Polls are political tools to promote a candidate. Nothing more. It will be fun.

My friend is brilliant, but like others, he's connected to the oil industry; he couldn't accept my big picture.

This Saudi prince had nothing to do with my original source, but he verified part of the plot. He was a prince delivering the check for the oil reserve purchase. He understood the game. When asked why they choose the United States for the oil reserve, he gave an American answer, "The United States is one of few nations that still have a rule of [oligarch's] law."

On October 10, 2020, the Internet carried the news that Attorney General William Barr was going to be able to review the election results for voter fraud. That set the stage for President Trump to try to interfere with the election results.

Then, Justice Samuel Alito, a George W. Bush appointee, asked for Pennsylvania to separate the ballots that came in after November 3.

Trump spoke at 2 AM on November 4, 2020, the eve of the election. He said he wanted to halt voting and have the Supreme Court review the election for fraudulent voting. He also wanted to be declared the winner. Trump was setting the stage for his lie about fraudulent votes.

The fix was in, but my main advisor assured me Biden's margin would prove too large. Gradually, I got more comfortable as the results came in, especially when Biden gained an 81,000 vote lead in Pennsylvania and Trump's people could only find 10,000 votes to complain about.

I did months of Facebook research. The intelligence people were very involved in social media supporting Trump. The people with mafia connections also expended a continuous effort to support Donald Trump. From the past, I knew several members of both groups who posted after me. I don't want to call names or go into the detail, but some were related.

Everyone got too biased on Facebook. The Mafia guys came in after the CIA people, and I got threats from both groups.

If you were committed to either party, and I came to you with evidence that your candidate was a crook or child molester, it wouldn't change your mind. You don't care what someone else said. Your mind was made up.

I understand. I once supported Nixon. It took me years to realize Nixon had flaws. He did the China deal perfectly, but he was very flawed. Hunter Thompson wrote about Nixon's character; he was on to Nixon.

Events didn't follow the GOP's Plan A script. There was to be a major coup to be blamed on the Democrats, but when Biden was elected, SCOTUS wouldn't hear the suits. That left Trump and his grade B lawyers floundering around in neverland denying Trump had lost.

When former Senate Majority Leader Mitch McConnell compared the people wanting the $2,000 stimulus to the greedy rich, he gave the Georgia votes to the Democrats. The Democrats won the two senate seats.

After that, there was no way Democrats would riot. They got everything handed them. The loss of senate seats in Georgia took the spark out of the real coup, but a tertiary event also factored in. A potential war with Iran didn't matter anymore, and I had a confirmation of that. The Allied forces had conquered the Middle-East, so if Biden won, that was irrelevant.

One could tell by how the Palestinians were kicked around and how Iraq was told to shut up after the Iranian general was murdered. The squeeze-down was on. Saudi dropped their oil production on January 5, 2021 a million barrels a day and Russia was allowed to sell more oil. The price of crude went to over $50 a barrel. The Saudis began dumping their excess in U.S. storage. Oil should stay in demand. You can't run a war with electric tanks and planes.

Poor old Donald Trump couldn't grasp the shifting wind. The oligarchs failed to communicate this to Trump or Trump didn't listen. Trump had his lawyers prepare a case for Ken Paxton, the Texas Attorney General, to allow Paxton to take the case directly to the Supreme Court. They hoped to overturn the vote in four states that Biden won. The Supreme Court rejected the argument by not allowing Texas to interfere in the elections in other states. Paxton may have also been seeking a pardon for himself because he was being investigated.

On December 6, security let the rioters into the Congressional buildings. Some intelligence people knew what was going to happen. The Republican sheep broke into Congress. A female QAnon member and a few others died. The fiasco eventually was blamed on the opportunists – Trump and Cruz.

Across the country, the Democrats laughed their asses off. The big third stimulus check might be coming and the GOP would take the blame. Trump was defeated. Someday someone will write a book: *It worked good until it didn't.*

The sentiment lingers; "Next time we'll bring real guns." The coup and QAnon may hang around. Once the military makes a plan, it's a long-term strategy. They're committed. But, now that the military has total control, the authorities will arrest a few people to make this look spontaneous. It may look like things have changed, but that's part of the game. QAnon has folded into the background.

The oligarchs are at the cusp of running a one-world society. How would one replace the oligarchs' political supporters? Before you try to answer, consider this QAnon post:

Royal Flush from Candace Owens:

"At the moment POTUS is sitting on a stack of Trump cards that he is waiting to unleash ... a royal flush! He has court cases that will go to the Supreme Court and thanks to the Texas case, he's now aware of how to file them properly ... under article 3 not 2 ... so SCOTUS will be forced to listen…….

He now has the DNI report. Barr stepped down and can now be a witness. He did his job. Durham is special counsel and can prosecute, in any state…. He's letting civil, criminal, and federal courts fail to handle this situation properly….so he can use military tribunals. He has ALL the data from the

NSA, the Kraken supercomputer and likely many more computers unknown to us.

He has the dueling electors from 7 state legislatures. He has VP Pence as the final arbiter of which ballots to accept….. He has the Insurrection Act, the NDDA, the national emergency, the 14th amendment, the 2018 executive order, the 2017 very first EO, the Patriot Act, the FISA warrants, the Declassification of everything, people swearing affidavits by the 1000s. He has all the statistical data being analyzed along with the video, emails, phone calls and bank transfer statements…..showing the coordination of the coup d'etat. He has RICO and he has the crimes against humanity videos. Wikileaks just dropped extensive information and Assange will be pardoned. Assange can then openly discuss the murder of Seth Rich….Now that the governors and secretary of states certified and Biden accepted…..they each committed and knowingly agreed to acts of Treason…..Solar Winds was literally just raided and Dominion is closing down, as well. He has the CIA servers used to change Dominion machine votes from Trump to Biden… he will soon have access to the actual machines, themselves….

He baited the Deep State into staying in DC, so they can be arrested. Biden hasn't accepted any transition money and Harris has still not given up her seat on the senate…..

The military has infiltrated Antifa and BLM. He has all their financial records. He knows which politicians took Chinese and Soros money, both Republican and Democrat…..He positioned Christopher Miller as secretary of defense and Ezra Cohen Watnick as assistant secretary of defense……with men loyal to him. The military has been flying planes far more than usual, all over the country. The navy just parked mega fleets on both coasts. The 82nd Airborne is preparing for an operation…..which has the same group that General Flynn & AG Donoghue were enlisted…

Pieces are falling into place. POTUS has it all. He is just laying out the pieces and building the narrative. He knows he won and they committed Treason! He set a trap and they walked right in, without hesitation.

He gave the Deep State the chance to come clean and try to fix things. They chose Treason! They will all hang as the result. Patriots in control! Nothing can stop what's coming.

The Storm is here!"

Yes, indeed - the storm and rioters were here. It took months to write this summary of the script, and wasn't it nice to see Mitch McConnell stick his fork in Ted Cruz as Cruz opened the door for the Bushes to get back in the game.

Let's revisit my story from where I first heard of the possibility of a coup, where I neither understood it or thought it was possible.

I heard Biden would win, but SCOTUS would reverse the results. Then the Democrats would riot and their coup would be crushed. I remember asking, "Does this mean the military is involved?" The answer I got was, "Yes," but I didn't buy in.

By October 8, 2020, I had a partial confirmation of this plan from the Saudi prince's rumor, but I didn't link the two stories. If Biden and SCOTUS overturned the vote and gave it to Trump, that would be the George W. Bush script, but I didn't connect the two conversations.

As I laid in bed one night looking at the ceiling, it did occur to me that this was the kind of information one should share with the authorities, but the first guy I was talking to is truthful only about 60% of the time. He knows you cannot repeat the story unless you warn others that it may not be true. His rumor mill is kind of like Trump's.

By now, you know I firmly believe the FBI is run by the CIA. There was no way I could share this with anyone.

In the end, what occurred was conditioned by the election results. If the election had been close, it could have gone to the Supreme Court, and I believe they could have given the election to Trump. Then, the Democrats would have been very upset. That might have caused a coup where the Democrats would have been slaughtered. As it was, the events forced the Republicans to go to plan B, where the QAnon nimrods were encouraged by the President to march on Congress.

That's when I realize the rumors I heard were true. I changed the title of this book and added my shaded details. I love how Plan B purged Trump and Cruz. Wasn't it sweat how Comey came in and wanted to just give Trump a slap on the wrist?

The oligarchs no longer needed Trump once they had control of the Middle East. It will be easier to influence Biden and Harris. Trump was too authoritarian.

I'm sure our allies, the Chinese, Russians, and the rest, have the big picture. Yes, the military was involved. Early on, they announced to the public that they would not get involved because that was not their role, but after the abortive coup attempt, they came out with a formal letter that it was their duty to protect the Constitution. These self-servers play the role of protecting you by saving the f%$king, antique Constitution. I always immediately think, "You're trying to justify your expensive jobs and retirement programs. If I have the story, then you created it."

The CIA brought the script to the military; the military approved it. The Democrats could have been the donkey, but in Plan B the QAnon sheep were the losers. Because of the events, only a few gullible followers were given 15 minutes of notoriety. It's a pity the U.S. doesn't have a re-educational facility like China. We need a school for guys like the Arkansas person wearing the buffalo horns.

If Plan A had worked, the oligarchs could take over and elections wouldn't be needed. We could get rid of fake democracy. Trump could have been replaced by Kushner.

The options on this script are limited. Remember, it was just a question of who profits from what occurs.

When Jack Kennedy was assassinated, someone remarked that it wasn't a conspiracy, just a lone nut who shot the president; the United States was therefore not a third-world country.

I beg your pardon! The Washington coup proves the United States is a third-world country. Yes, we are QAnon!

Rule 12: The oligarchs write powerful scripts that they adjust to take advantage of the nimrods. They can't stay at the top any other way.

The GOP, the CIA, the mafias, the religions, and the media backs the oligarch's play.

Today's groups are bonded slime-balls, and the people they appoint are the apples that didn't fall far from the tree. Use your connections and imagination to avoid getting sucked into their intrigue; or just ask me!

The Jewish Syndicate

I was a mule with blinders because there were no admitted Jews in Fayetteville. Until 2020, I didn't realize why not all Jews were Zionists. Zionists are defined by a political view and Jews are defined by their Judean religious beliefs.

What follows is what experience has taught me. To augment my education, I did read Andrew Carrington Hitchcock's *The Synagogue of Satan*, which is a biased book sold on the website AndrewCarringtonHitchcock.com.

The Jewish story begins around 740 AD, but they achieved a major presence when the Rothschilds became the first family of international money lenders. In 1812, Mayer Amschel Rothschild's famous statement was, "Give me control of a nation's money, and I care not who makes its laws."

In the U.S., the public needs to communicate and solve its issues. Diversity is a hindrance to truth, but the public has little commonality. As a result, diversity is encouraged by the most clannish groups. In the case of the Jewish Syndicate, it's easier to rule if the Gentiles are diversified.

The Jewish oligarchs succeed because they are better organized; they more effectively use monopolies, inside information, and credit. "Classified" and secret information are most important. Those who have access to significant information and credit have position to make less-risky wagers in the markets. In 1815, Rothschild made a fortune betting on early news of the Duke of Wellington's victory over Napoleon Bonaparte at Waterloo. When the blood flowed in the streets, he placed his wagers.

Insider information translated into wagers is at the heart of the U.S. money trail. There you find the FED, a private bank authorized to manage the financial soundness of the United States.

In 1910, Nelson Aldrich and executives, representing the banks of J.P. Morgan, Rockefeller, and Kuhn, Loeb & Co., secluded themselves for ten days at Jekyll Island, Georgia. Their plan was to authorize a government bank they could privately control.

Disclosure of the meetings came three years after the Federal Reserve Act was passed when journalist Bertie Charles Forbes wrote a 1916 article about the "hunting trip." Warburg defended the secret meetings, saying the participants were engaged in patriotic work by trying to correct weaknesses of the U.S. banking system.

Warburg's plan advocated a private monopoly with little government influence. President Wilson named Warburg and other prominent experts to direct the new system, which began operations in 1915. **The FED is a privately-owned U.S. central bank with authorization to print money. The FED inflates and deflates the money supply. They print money and charge interest. The FED works with the IRS to make sure the public pays them interest on the debt they create.**

Paul Warburg had ties to J.P. Morgan and his daughter was married to John D. Rockefeller Jr. Eventually, **the FED was controlled by the Rockefellers, who were the most powerful family in the world. In 1932 the Rockefellers took over the J.P. Morgan flagship bank, the Chase.**

John D. Rockefeller's concept of business was, "Competition is a sin." He **built** a monopoly in the **oil industry. His success began when the Standard Oil companies cornered the oil refinery markets. Exxon was later formed by the merger of Humble Oil and Mobil, two oil companies the Rockefellers had interests in.**

The Rockefellers as oligarchs created a financial empire by controlling the FED and the richest bank in America, Chase Bank. Rockefellers had access to classified information through Chase, the FED, their CFR and oil company connections, and day-to-day contacts with high ranking military and political officials, people like Allen and John Foster Dulles.

The Rockefellers also had access to FBI Director J. Edgar Hoover and his powerful network. It was Hoover who warned Nelson Rockefeller that Alger Hiss was a communist spy. [Y30] That information was used by Nelson to elevate the public recognition of Richard Nixon.

The Rockefellers initiated major financial strategies. They closely collaborated with what I refer to as the Jewish Syndicate - the Jewish elites, oligarchs, the Mossad, and the Jewish mafia. The Jewish clan acts as a group. Volunteer Jewish helpers have a bond to Israel that exceeds any allegiance to the United States. The Jewish ethos is to do what is right for Mossad and Israel. [Y31]

The Jewish Syndicate instills the belief that they are smarter than other clans. They feel entitled to avoid sweaty jobs by providing most of the lawyers and accountants to run the government and other industries. Through their unions, they control actors and actresses, service workers, teachers, and others. They focus on leading and therefore their clan occupies the highest paying jobs and the jobs that allow them to influence what occurs, especially in industries their clan dominates.

The Jewish Syndicate includes the FED investors. Although the Syndicate's power is vested in multiple revenue-generating areas, their primary strength comes from the Fed's ability to establish the strength of the U.S. dollar.

A larger percentage of FED Chairmen have been Jewish. President Reagan brought in Alan Greenspan as FED chairman. Greenspan had been a member of Morgan Guaranty Trust Company, part of the Morgan-Rockefeller interests. His predecessor Paul Volcker also served the Rockefeller interests. [Y32] Another example, Janet Yellen was from Brooklyn. She studied under Joseph Stiglitz at Yale.

Besides printing currency and controlling interest rates, the FED can put a floor under the price of commodities like oil and natural gas. They work with the major oil companies and the IMF to accomplish their goals.

The FED snares the public and other nations as debt slaves. The FED serves its owners while the masses are led to believe in 401Ks and the stock market.

In recent years, the over-supply of fiat money coupled with low-interest rates forced pensioners and savers to invest their savings in stocks. The good stuff, the insider information, like the future strength of the dollar, is left to the Fed's investors, while the public is forced to gamble against market manipulators.

Jewish workers aggressively seek better-paying jobs that control industries. Jewish workers want class distinction and the highest paying jobs. Isn't that the reason most of the U.S. sports commissioners are Jewish?

At a young age, many Jewish people are mature enough to pick up on the concepts of elitism and business management. They may have early exposure to law and investments as a result of their clan's focus, which is used for banking, entertainment, and the financial markets. When companies are taken public, their stock value rises five-fold, and often it is a Jewish firm involved with the underwriting.

Many Jewish people only have Jewish friends, unless the other party has money. Some Jewish people do not make non-Jewish friends unless there is some possible business relationship that has potential rewards. Jewish people in general go out of their way to avoid all non-Jewish connections. They also will use other Jewish firms even if they are not competitive. They keep the money in the clan.

Other clans [Amish, Mormon, Italian, Irish, Chinese, African Americans, German, Baptist, etc.] are also partial to their groups, but they're not as effectively focused. The Jewish Syndicate concentrates on their specialty areas, which enhance the clan's power. Jewish lawyers dominate the legal industry because it is at the heart of the Capitalist system. They control the stock market, politics, and unions. They also focus on the medical industry because the pay is exceptional.

I was an officer in a public computer company. Our group sued a group of Dallas elites over a large facilities management contract. Included in the other group was Trammel Crow, the large builder.

We used a Jewish law firm. Our Dallas law firm brought in a Philadelphia [Jewish] law firm for support. One of the Philadelphia lawyers was a young lawyer named Leonard Barrack. Not yet 30, Barrack had never lost a suit or settled for less than a million dollars. In later years, Barrack went on to win at least one billion-dollar lawsuit.

In our suit, we thought we had Trammel Crow nailed. After about 30 minutes on the stand, Barrack asks Crow a critical question. Crow responded with an adverse answer. Barrack changed the dialog and then spent 30 minutes navigating around to the other side of the question. When Barrack asked Crow the same question from a different perspective, Crow responded as we had hoped, completely the opposite from his prior testimony. Barrack then spent 20 minutes moving the subject to another topic before letting Crow off the stand.

Barrack won the suit for us, but it took years. It proved to me people can lie under oath if they are well-coached by great lawyers.

The Jewish Syndicate will buy influence if possible. Gore Vidal and Alexander Cockburn reported it became common knowledge in DC political circles that during the desperate days of Truman's underdog 1948 reelection campaign, Truman secretly accepted a cash payment of $2M from wealthy Zionists in exchange for recognizing Israel. [Y33]

The Jewish clan is so heavily involved with organized crime that as a clan they have to be considered a mafia. In the 1920s, the mafias controlled the clubs in New York, Chicago, Detroit, and other big northern cities. It was a different game because of the Depression and illegal booze.

In the 1930s, the Mafia controlled gambling. Their betting line came out of St. Louis where they controlled the communication workers' union. Hoover's FBI couldn't and wouldn't stop that. Hoover was addicted to betting the horses, and he loved getting his tips on fixed races.

The Italian Mafia was sometimes the assassination arm and the Jewish Syndicate might represent the accounting and legal arm. Al Capone had several Jewish employees in high positions.

Jewish gangsters like Arnold Rothstein, Sam Bronfman, Meyer Lansky, Morris "Moe" Dalitz, and Benjamin "Bugsy" Siegel controlled their equivalent of Mafia families. The Meyer Lansky and Bugsy Siegel group in New York had a team of top hitmen. When Arnold Rothstein reorganized the crime networks, the Bugs and Lansky hit team evolved into Murder Inc, a contract murder group to kill "free enterprise" groups who thought they could buck the crime syndicate.

Murder Inc killed hundreds of people. They operated like a Mafia police force. J. Edgar Hoover couldn't stop Murder Inc. Hoover and his FBI would have been destroyed if he had taken on Murder Inc. Instead, Hoover had his agents investigate communists.

I talked with a Jewish gentleman [Mr. X] in Atlantic City who knew Meyer Lansky. His father did work for Lansky. He said Lansky was greatly respected in the community. Lansky always did profitable deals. He advised friends where to buy a home or invest, and they always made money.

When Mr. X was about 12, he got to talk with Mr. Lansky, and he asked Lansky how he avoided J. Edgar Hoover. Lansky told him Hoover called him on the phone; "Lansky, I've got the goods on you. I can throw you in jail or have you deported." Hoover probably recruited a lot of snitches like Whitey Bolger using that line.

In his best little girl's voice, Lansky responded, "Well, Mr. Hoover, why don't you come over and show me your evidence?"

Hoover and Clyde Tolson came by Lansky's offices. Hoover laid out his evidence. In a little girl's voice, Lansky said, "Well, I have some evidence for you." Lansky took out a picture and laid it on the table. It showed J. Edgar giving a blow-job. [The CIA had a similar picture of Hoover - probably a duplicate.]

As Tolson leaned for a closer look, Lansky put a second picture on the table. "I have one for you too, Mr. Tolson."

Tolson wore a grass skirt in a compromising position.

Hoover: "What do you want?" Lansky: "We don't exist."

When Robert Kennedy reviewed Hoover's list of Mafia bosses, he asked, "Why isn't Lansky on this list?"

"He's not Italian [, and besides, he has a picture of me]."

In 2020, after the collapse of the markets and the stimulus package that brought a temporary recovery, the FED was criticized for helping the rich with policies that failed to trickle down to the labor markets. Sheila Bair, former head of the FDIC, said that after the 2008 financial crisis, "it took 10 years for lower- and middle-income families to see gains."

Bair criticized the interest rate policy of the FED as the driver of inequality. Bair went on to say, "If they are going to heat up the printing press, where is the money going now? It's going into financial markets, benefitting banks and large corporations that use the bond markets to fund themselves." [Y34]

Sure, give the middle- and lower-classes $1,200 when they should have gotten over $14,000, and give the rich the money so they can buy stocks and bonds. That will run the markets up and help get the President re-elected!

In 2013, I went to Biloxi and stayed at the Beau Rivage for Super Bowl weekend. The Society of Miscreants, to which I belonged, used the occasion to eat fine seafood, gamble, play golf at the Fallen Oak golf course, and enjoy the arts and entertainment of the Gulf Coast.

I rode to the Fallen Oak golf course with two Jewish brothers. One was the obligatory lawyer son and the other was the doctor son. Both were highly successful.

I knew where our conversation was going. I threw out the bait. "Well, what do you think about Iran?"

"Don't worry about them. We've got the bunker busters waiting." The brothers viewed the U.S. military as their Jewish army.

Any non-Jewish person who offers a comment on the Middle East problems, be it constructive or not, he will probably be ostracized and labeled as anti-Semitic. That may be true even if his opinion agrees with Israel. The person offering constructive opinions may even be Jewish, like comedian Mort Sahl. Mort Sahl tried to solve the JFK assassination. That was too close to home. It was public knowledge that Israel wanted nuclear weapons and Jack Kennedy wouldn't give in.

The entertainment industry was dominated by Jewish and Italian mafias, and Sahl quickly got to where he couldn't find work. The Jewish clan didn't want to hear Sahl's assassination opinions.

The location of Israel creates problems. As of the last count, there were less than a dozen Christians left in Egypt - millions have had to flee the Middle East because of the Jewish culture. The Middle East conflict has made the world more dangerous.

Many in the U.S. community oppose the expansion of settlements in Palestinian territories, but the Israeli hard-liners press forward to have their people re-inhabit the desert-like land. The Zionists never had any intention of returning any confiscated land.

The Jewish Syndicate takes the United States for granted. Do the Israelis believe dropping a few bombs will allow Israel to retain the last 1,000 acres of arid desert land they took from the Arabs? No! This is all about racial hatred and religion. Religion is a class definition all about control.

The Jewish controlled FED has a similar purpose as unions. After the Federal Reserve Act passed, President Woodrow Wilson had regrets: "I have unwittingly ruined my country. ... No longer a government of free opinion, no longer a government of conviction and the vote of the majority, but a government by the opinion and duress of a small group of dominant men."

Wilson gave too much power to the Federal Reserve owners. There was no transparency. The name Federal was a lie. Wilson had been snookered!

Jack Kennedy understood and was going to replace the Federal Reserve. He knew the Jewish elites controlled the FED and indirectly the U.S., but the oligarchs terminated his quest.

The Jewish clan and the U.S. military develop financial games and play them exceptionally well. As an example, Japan was not supposed to control the United States financially, but by 1990 the Japanese had made serious inroads into the U.S. economy.

Beginning at the end of WW II, the Japanese functioned as the design and manufacturing arm for U.S. high technology. They got to where they eventually controlled the design of the more complex hardware. As a result, the Japanese economy grew so strong it allowed the Japanese to begin buying prime property in the United States, everything from the Pebble Beach golf course to the Rockefeller Center in New York.

The Allied group had to take Japan down a peg. I had a friend whose uncle was an ambassador. One evening at a dinner in Austin, my friend was asked his opinion of Japan. He said that he thought Japan would continue to excel. Immediately afterward his uncle pulled him aside and told him, "We are going to break Japan. It's got where we can't compete with them."

Supposedly, former CIA director William Colby was his uncle's source. Colby had become an ambassador.

Some wars are financial wars. In 1985, Treasury Secretary Jim Baker did a secret deal with West Germany, Japan, France, and the UK. Signed at the Plaza Hotel in New York, the agreement was referred to as the Plaza Accord. It called for the depreciation of the U.S. dollar in relation to the Japanese Yen and the German Deutsche Mark. The value of the dollar relative to the other currencies fell 50% over the next few years, and it continued to fall for over a decade, well into Bill Clinton's term.

David Rockefeller took advantage of the strengthening yen. In 1989, Rockefeller Center Inc. sold 80% of its interests to Mitsubishi Estate Corporation for $1.373 billion.

After the yen was over-strengthened, the Japanese stock market collapsed. David Rockefeller commented, "Alas, in the end, the purchase of RCI proved to be a nightmare for the Japanese. ... By mid-1990 demand had flattened and it was difficult to retain tenants at $35 a square foot." [Y35]

David Rockefeller struck a deal with Goldman's Whitehall Realty for 50% ownership in a joint venture to repurchase Rockefeller Center. He wrote, "A Rockefeller once again owns the crown jewel, not only of New York but the nation."

The English try to moderate and balance the international scene so they can remain in power. They do this in conjunction with a strong Jewish influence. Many wealthy Jewish entrepreneurs from America move back to London after they have made it. J. Paul Getty was an example and Gerald Hines was another. Hines was raised in Houston. He developed the Galleria and the Shell complex before moving to London.

Hines maintains a construction operation in Houston. A few years ago, I played golf with the father-in-law of Lars, the person running Hines' construction operation in Houston, so I have a small picture. Also, my father set up quail hunts for E.E. Townes, one of the founders of the Humble Company. Townes told my father how he unsuccessfully tried to recruit Hines before Hines launched into the construction business.

U.S. intelligence has a long relationship with the Jewish Syndicate and the English, and their collusion and the huge technical resources required in today's world are destroying entrepreneurship. For example, when the CIA sold their mapping company to Google, they sold a business that taxpayers had invested billions of dollars in. Does anyone believe the CIA didn't retain an influential interest in Google?

When Google purchased YouTube, they took control of the largest segment of the publishing industry, which is directed at influencing the masses. YouTube dictates what the majority of the world views. Do you think YouTube's interests correspond to Google's interests, which correspond to the CIA's interests?

YouTube controls what the public sees. Google will be first on the list to get any government-related business.

YouTube guidelines prevent posting spam, scams, harmful content, pornography, sexually explicit videos, threats, and hateful content. [Y36]

Do you think Google would allow anyone to publish a story that reflects negatively on the CIA? Wouldn't it disappear into the too-anti-establishment waste-basket?

The elites' corporations get loans from the government and/or they receive large government contracts. Legal and financial connections help. Frequently the CEO will be Jewish. Go down the list - Google [Sergey Brin, Larry Page], Oracle [Larry Ellison], Dell [Michael Dell], Facebook [Mark Zuckerberg], Microsoft [Steven Ballmer], Apple [Steve Jobs], etc.

And even though Jeffrey Bezos is not written up as being Jewish, he was born as Jeffrey Preston Jorgensen. Did you count those five "es"?

In 1993, Bezos started an online book store named Amazon. In 2000, Bezos funded Blue Origin, a spaceflight startup company. Did the elites ask Bezos to found Blue Origin or was that his idea?

Bezos also made several billion as an original shareholder of Google. Amazon and Google regularly participate in deals and receive government contracts.

As a result of the confluence of elites' power, there are more and more billion-dollar contracts supported by investment firms, which feature principals with military connections. For example, there was a billion-dollar solar plant built in New Jersey. The NJ solar facility has massive software support. It used three levels of software security.

This solar project supplies weather information and is connected to other large software systems. This project was guaranteed by the U.S. government. If it loses money, the taxpayers will cover the losses. If it makes money, the owners, who include officials with intelligence connections, will profit.

Financiers will always profit, and the taxpayers will take the risk. Elon Musk isn't totally financing his risky deals. Taxpayers help Musk!

I was asked in February 2018 if I was aware of an oil service company named Quintana Energy Services, QES. The person making the query said QES was being taken public at a reduced price because the DOW fell 10%.

I replied, "No, but let me guess. QES is a $300M corporation and they are being taken public by Goldman Sachs."

"I think they gross about $320M, but I don't know if Goldman is an underwriter."

Goldman was not taking QES public, but QES was on Goldman's recommended buy list.

At the time Goldman dominated the oil services space and the appropriate revenue amount for an oil services company to be taken public is about $300M per year. QES went public around $9 a share. When oil collapsed in 2020, QES fell to $.69.

Big trading firms find it difficult to separate their interests from fiduciary responsibility. A decade ago, Goldman was fined for sub-prime trading activities.

Carmen Segara, a former NY FED expert examiner, wrote *Noncompliant: A Lone Whistleblower Exposes the Giants of Wall Street*. Her book explains how the FED works to expand Jewish influence by giving special treatment to firms like Goldman. Goldman gets rewarded instead of being reprimanded.

Stock market collusion is one of the reasons the U.S. has gone from doing 95% of the venture capital deals to doing 50% of the deals in the last three decades. The $500M deals now have 20% of the market, or around 80 deals a year. [Y37] There are fewer middle-class deals.

The elites' Deep State controls the government's budget and they use the public's money to enslave the masses. The conservative GOP elites make sure there is no money to support moderate media people who would address major issues.

The Jewish Syndicate can't allow their agenda to be compromised by the truth. In 1843, B'nai B'rith was set up by the Jews in New York City as a Masonic Lodge. Seven decades later they established the Anti-Defamation League. The ADL espouses the concept of anti-Semitism. If you get accused of their term anti-Semitic, it should be a sufficient response, "But, I am not racist." The inference of that would be, "but you are."

The ADL is a racist organization. The public should shut down ADL or make it support all clans. There is no reason to be partial. The ADL needs to answer why they think the Jewish Syndicate is superior, and why the Zionists should run the U.S.

The Jewish Syndicate and the Catholics are experts at coordinating with mafias. This is a natural connection. They both should offer an explanation why the ADL isn't shut down and why they think they need to run the country. Why does the U.S. need two groups that are raping the country?

All religions and the public needs to debate this because society needs better parity. This is probably why Assange went to jail. He got too close to the truth.

We need fewer Jewish lawyers and mafia-controlled unions. A law eliminating Jewish lawyers in Washington and as union leaders for the next 30 years would help level the playing field and send a message.

Removing all the Jewish lawyers from the DOJ, FBI, military, and Hollywood could also help. The United States should nationalize the FED and use Native American lawyers to put a little honor back in the system. This is not punishment being discussed. Who ran the decision-making process that failed? Who got the money and the better-paying jobs?

This subject can't be addressed properly without looking at the role of the aggressive CIA which operates as a government mafia immune from prosecution.

Rule 13: The hypocrisy of Christianity and Judaism is a subject a citizen should understand. The clannish groups are racist and their collusion distorts the social structures.

Our Allied Partners

The monarchies, the kings and queens, were the oligarchs, but they were like the Muslims in Iran - not inclusive enough. They were dethroned and a new group of opportunists funded politicians to run the government. The new oligarchs faded into the background and became back-seat drivers - puppeteers.

During WW II, U.S. naval intelligence and the mafias worked as one. After WW II, Lansky's partner, Lucky Luciano, was released from prison and the Italian mafia was reestablished in Italy, Corsica, and Sicily.

The military-mafia relationship is still in place - an unholy alliance between the [Catholic-Italian] Mafia, the Jewish clan, and the Allied intelligence agencies. This agreement to work together has allowed the Jewish, Italian, and Anglo mafia chiefs to dominate gambling and entertainment in the Allied countries. These groups work together because smuggling drugs and guns, laundering money, and avoiding taxes have always been prized talents of the oligarchs.

Every press release mentioning our allies closes with a statement that the U.S. will always support our allies. Our allies are part of the U.S. elites. England and its former colonies are our greatest allies. The English Anglos have a close relationship with the Jewish elites. They work together to support and influence the U.S., and vice versa. The U.S. supported England's Falkland war. In turn, Tony Blair, derided as "Bush's poodle", supported Bush's Iraq war. [Y38]

Five Eyes is a perfect example of the British-US relationship. The Pentagon was created as the head of the Western intelligence alliance, the core of which was an Anglo group of countries referred to as "Five Eyes." The participating countries were America, England, Canada, Australia, and New Zealand. [Y39] We trust them and they trust us.

Five Eyes, the U.S.-British code group, was charged with protecting coded communications. In 2012, Canadian navy officer Jeffrey Delisle was arrested for passing secrets to Moscow. Delisle worked for Five Eyes. As a mole, he offered the Russians our communications coding secrets, but the Russians were only interested in the small stuff. [Y40]

The Russians must have already had the most important intelligence. Were the Russians given the code secrets by the United States? And if the U.S. is a partner with the Russians, then wouldn't the U.S. also be a partner with China?

Did Russians and Chinese elites give us their secrets so we wouldn't have conflicts, outside of the normal phony acts that get staged? How many spies were caught in the last twenty years?

Power is more concentrated than ever, and the super-powers can't afford to forfeit their power. Why shouldn't the U.S. elite collude with their adversaries? It's an insurance policy.

Regardless of the adversarial competition, the Allied elites would rather not allow another super-power to fail. It would put stress on their game.

When the Russian economy faltered, the U.S. helped Russia enhance its oil production. Brown & Root built the pipeline from Russia to Europe. My deceased in-law said he helped negotiate approval with the Russian mafia. "How much do we have to pay you to allow us to build a pipeline to Europe?"

I'm sure Brown & Root tacked the charge on their bill.

The potential of the three super-powers like the U.S., China, and Russia having a conflict is scary. At least they are separated by oceans, and mutual financial investments causes them to want to avoid major confrontations.

The super-elites operate with similar agendas, especially if they are partners. With the Allied group partnered with Russia, it was easy for them to collude and kill ISIS fundamentalists. It helps when someone recovers a flash drive with the names of 22,000 foreign supporters.

I suspect Russia, China, and the U.S. would not want to show up as a group and support the same objective. It might be too obvious that they have similar interests. That meant Russia had to back Assad. It's a very concept. All of this is a joint coordinated strategy to fool the sheep.

Non-super-power nations directly or indirectly follow one of the super-powers. Syrian President Bashar al-Assad commented, "The Americans will put you in their pockets so you can be tools in the barter."

That's how the system works. Take the British. They're tied to the U.S.

The Chinese Communist Party is not like the Soviet Communist Party. They're not McDonald's franchises. Ethos and quality control are different. Chinese customs, holidays, games, and society are different.

Brown people working with white Russians? Are you serious? The Chinese may have hired a Russian assassin to take care of that antiquities dealer I wrote of, but that was a small, isolated instance.

No nation is honest or sophisticated enough to run a pure democracy. Even the U.S. public didn't appreciate it when they had a democracy. Democracy is too easily pushed aside by nationalistic greed or a bad economy.

Arab Spring, democracy! The Arabs can't envision democracy. All they want is their daily bread. I've talked with troops who spoke multiple Middle East languages. Middle East democracy is a fantasy. Women are second-class citizens.

There's no pure Communism or pure Capitalism left. Russia and China are twenty-first-century dictatorships with socialism for the rich, like the U.S. and England.

The super-powers are at a crossing in the road. China, Russia, and the U.S. have some degree of military parity, enough bombs to kill each other. In China's case, they have developed carrier-killer missiles in an attempt to counter the U.S.'s carrier fleet.

Our partner, Russia, seems tired of playing the adversary role. They warned the U.S. of their dooms-day line in the sand. If that statement was correct, the same could be said for China. Fortunately, this should be just a game. The super-power elites will play their game as long as they can fool the masses.

The one world game has run for 75 years, and the Allied oligarchs hope they can get an amicable deal in place so the oligarchs can continue to control the world. The world no longer needs more manufacturing capability. The world needs fewer people, politics, and military. The super-powers need to work together for financial and social balance.

Ray Dalio is the founder of the world's largest hedge fund, Bridgewater Associates. On October 26, 2020, Mr. Dalio was in an Internet interview discussing the phases the U.S. has gone through - the Grand Area strategy that went into effect at the end of WW II, the Nixon decision to not back our sovereign currency with gold, and the current situation with China, where the U.S. has essentially lost control of its finances.

Dalio was very general. Being a billionaire hedge fund operator, Dalio certainly understands finance and capitalism, but he can't visualize a system that would more fairly distribute global revenues. People like Dalio only think of their interests, and they do nothing to improve the social structure. Robert Kennedy Jr. also has a little of that problem. People with too much money live in glass houses.

Rule 14: See the long-term picture and separate yourself mentally from politics and clannish bias. The history of the Allied oligarchs needs to be judged. Sort out the Queen, the Pope, the mafias, the intelligence agencies, and the other players; otherwise, you will go through life as just another sheep. It's time to understand and participate!

Mafias, the CIA, and Drugs

In the old days the underworld was honorable. They had rules of fairness.

The head Mafia boss on Dago Hill near Brown University in Providence had the snowplow clear the whole street in front of his house; he regularly donated to the local church to let the community know everything was in solid hands.

During World War II a solder sent back some Christmas presents for his family. His wife had them in the trunk of her car. One day the trunk was pried open and all the presents were gone. She immediate drove up to Patriarca's laundry and told Raymond of her dilemma; Christmas was coming on and all her presents were stolen.

A day later, the trunk is pried open again and all the presents were there, except for two German Luger pistols her husband had included in the package.

Because of all the drugs and money, and the CIA, things have changed a lot. Wherever one finds the mafias, there will be drugs and money laundering to avoid taxes.

The religious organizations always expect the mafias and the CIA to support their existence. The CIA is a most powerful mafia because it is a legal mafia using taxpayer money.

The CIA is integral to society. It used to be the religions had the connection to the mafias. Now the intelligence community controls the mafias because their surveillance technology is so strong. It doesn't hurt to have immunity. If you are a doubter, read Douglas Valentine's *The CIA as Organized Crime*.

The individuals that take drugs may get addicted. In the least case, they become less productive because drugs impair one's ability to focus.

Drugs cause society in places like Hollywood to lose its direction. Screenwriters don't write good screenplays. They pay cheap foreign labor a few hundred dollars to write a screenplay. The screenplay is poor, but the rich and famous screenwriter will enhance the product until it becomes suitable for entertainment. There will be more action and not much of a real story, but it will make money for the producer because he just needs something surreal to plug into the media distribution network.

The Jewish Syndicate controlling Hollywood didn't want answers to social problems. Producers bow to the Motion Picture Academy to have their films put in the elites' distribution channels. The film industry produces irrelevant movies that can be profitable. This approach ruined the late-shows and comedy. Politically correct spokespeople lack the talent to tell funny jokes and carry on interesting conversations.

The major magazines are worse. They should also be required to do a more thought-provoking job. People always talk about television not having anything new, but magazines fail to offer articles with intellectual content. The Wall Street Journal, Harper's, and others seldom present cutting-edge analysis. They don't question non-celebrity writers who are experts on edgy subjects. They name-drop in no-brain articles.

The CIA has known how drugs control society for the last sixty years; they have taken over. In an early JFK assassination book, *Bloody Treason*, Author Noel Twyman asked the CIA operative Garry Patrick Hemming, "Who do you think was the [JFK assassination] mastermind? The one man who put it all together?" [Y41]

Hemming replied, "Hoover … Hoover was monitoring it so that at any point he could stop it …."

Twyman later asked about incentive: "The joint ventures of intelligence [CIA] and narcotics in siphoning off of money for covert operations - that money must stick to some people's hands personally too?"

Hemming was blunt, "That's the only incentive. You put your ass on the line … If you are a gun runner, you have an in at the palace level throughout the planet. If you are a doper, you have control of the palace level in every country throughout the planet." [Y42]

Hemming capsulated our situation, and John L. Potash's *Drugs as Weapons Against Us* is *the* landmark book to read. It reviews the early English and American oligarchs who made fortunes from drug smuggling. After some history of the drug wars, the book discusses how the CIA began using drugs to target the Panthers, Jimi Hendrix, Kurt Cobain, John Lennon, Malcolm X, MLK, Robert Kennedy, Che Guevara, and anyone they considered an activist. They were eliminating any competition.

When drugs were used to control an activist and that failed, then arrangements were made to kill him. If the CIA had to use Klaus Barbie to kill someone, they did! When an agency of the military kills a John Kennedy and a John Lennon, it empowers them. They have to control the media and the entire drug mechanism. This is the United States' unfortunate circumstance.

Other agencies like the FBI, DEA, and the Secret Service are trapped because they have to support the CIA's efforts. When necessary, agents used their intelligence membership to plead immunity. This is the most exciting game in the world. That makes it addictive. It is also dangerous because it is a violation of the law; the CIA was not authorized to operate domestically.

This is all justified by the Grand Area plans to make the Allied oligarchs the big dog – to control everything. As a result, the U.S. has the same cartel problems as Mexico. The CIA controls the flow of drugs in the U.S. To do so, they must maintain a handle on the mafias' activities.

If a person questions the CIA's involvement with drugs, eventually he will come down to this question: "Well, would you like someone else to be controlling drugs?" The CIA acts like this is unstoppable because it's the revenue source for their business model, and they have to use drugs as a weapon against activists and anyone who disagrees with their policies.

To make everything work, the CIA must influence the media in order for the public to ignore the drug problem. The public can't do anything about it because they will be killed if they try to intervene. It will not be surprising when people in the U.S. wind up employing vigilante justice like there is in Mexico.

In 2016, *Power Shift* was released by one of the world's leading international lawyers, Richard Falk. Falk has written about 30 books, and *Power Shift* reviews international power. It was praised by intellectuals at Yale Law School, the University of London, and the London School of Economics.

Power Shift's index has no mention of the Jewish or Italian mafia even though the mafias are still all-powerful. For instance, I met an ex-IBMer who rose to be a Senior Systems Engineer with IBM, the highest rank attainable in the technical career category.

Dr. Frank had a Ph.D. and had taught college in Chicago. One day, while administering a test, he caught Mrs. Guiseppe cheating. He called her aside and informed her he was going to fail her in the course, and she need not attend another class.

The next day, two well-dressed male specimens appear at the professor's room and inquired if he would consider reinstating Mrs. Guiseppe. They told him that her maiden name was Giancana, a very close relative of Sam Giancana, who ran the Chicago Mafia.

Dr. Frank told them he had passed the matter on to the dean, but he would [immediately] talk to the dean and see if the dean would reinstate her. Giancana's boys said that would be fine. They would contact the dean later in the day to see how that went. When they left, he called the dean and said, "You's got a problem!"

Mrs. Guiseppe was reinstated and placed in a class taught by another instructor.

Go to Wikipedia! The same old Mafia families run New York – Bonanno, Colombo, Genovese, Lucchese, and Gambino. The bosses are elites, and they are in bed with the DOJ! The mafias provide financial support for the President and all the politicians. The capitals are where those big yellow envelopes with the cash are left.

The Deep State includes the military, and the military includes the CIA. The CIA uses total surveillance to monitor and control everyone.

For decades, the military and the FBI supplied world-wide intelligence to the President and the Pentagon. The CIA had immunity and used sophisticated public monitoring equipment.

The CIA knows if you are going to vote and how you will vote. This puts the CIA in position to be the mafias' silent partner.

In the 1960s, because they were not supposed to operate domestically, the CIA had the rule to use contract mafia assassins in the U.S. The CIA also needed the mafia connections to control the flow of drug money. The CIA strongly bonded as mafia partners when they managed the JFK assassination.

The media don't identify the mafia bosses as elites because the mafias' assassins are used by the oligarchs. The mafia bosses are not criticized unless they get killed or are sent to jail.

The media and politicians pretend there are no lines between gambling and legitimate business. A Jewish casino owner like Sheldon Adelson could donate $25M or more to Donald Trump's campaign before Trump's 2016 election.

Years earlier, when Adelson wasn't allowed to control online gambling, he became opposed to online gambling. If he couldn't control online poker, it might adversely affect his

Las Vegas Sands Corporation because the Venetian casino had a large poker room. Online poker could take away some business. It's not just poker. Any online gambling would be competitive to the Las Vegas Sands.

On January 14, 2019, Trump's Justice Department ruled online gambling was illegal.

The Italians have their tomato-based pasta and olives and cheese, but they also have as industries the Catholic Church and the Mafia. The money the Catholic Church makes in the U.S. is sent back to Italy. The cash is not re-invested locally.

A 2020 article on drug smuggling defined how 300 Italian families controlled a good portion of the U.S. drug smuggling.

Interestingly, at the height of the Corona panic, U.S. Attorney General William Barr announced he is issuing an arrest warrant for Nicolas Maduro and a group of Venezuelan generals. They were supposedly involved in drug smuggling.

I wonder which lucky group will take over this drug chain. Who are the people capable of pulling this off? Are the conspirators the Catholics, mafias, Israelis, CIA, British, or all of the above? Or, will there be a payoff?

Religion and the mafias are ever-present in larger cities. Decades ago, my friend Tom Toland started in Dallas as a marketing person for IBM's Service Bureau Corporation. SBC would process a company's data and print the firm's reports. Tom was canvassing for new prospects and he came across a company with a warehouse full of pin ball machines and all sorts of equipment that went into nightclubs.

Tom talked with a person who appeared to be the manager and he seemed interested in SBC's services. At the end of Tom's presentation, another person came in and he appeared to be the higher manager. He asked what Tom was doing there. As his lower-level manager explained the services SBC was offering, the upper manager told Tom to leave, to "get out."

Tom accommodated. Later he learned the company was owned by Carlos Marcello and they supplied the equipment to all the clubs in Dallas and Ft. Worth. The Louisiana Mafia had taken over Dallas. They loaned money to set up clubs. If you didn't use their services, you could expect to find a screwdriver hole punched through the mother-board of whatever equipment you were using. The message was clear and direct.

This Mafia based monopoly was the reason Carlos Marcello could afford to donate $500,000 to Lyndon Johnson's campaign.

The CIA is the reason the U.S. has 100 bases in foreign countries and greedy schemers profit from selling weapons and drugs to other countries. The mafias and the CIA should have been scattered in the winds in the 1960s and 1970s, but the Kennedys were assassinated. Now, because of digital technology, the public again has the opportunity to eliminate the underworld.

The CIA and NSA work with the Jewish Syndicate to control the media. They make "fake news" the central theme. For instance, the lies of the century - Pearl Harbor, the JFK assassination, the Liberty ship attack, and 9-11 - were never solved for the public because the truth would point to the elites.

Intellectuals used to define the public's complex social structure. Real intellectuals no longer exist because the oligarchs will not allow outsiders any voice.

The JFK assassination was the starting message - don't pull an end-run. The Catholics were left to console their flock, as they always do: "Jack Kennedy's assassination was what God had meant to be."

The Catholics and Israelis have now re-partnered to run the Allied world. They work together, even though it seems they work separately. The Catholic never out the Israelis in the media, and vice-versa.

The horse the masses have in this race is the future generation. Everyone deserves the right to consider their future and voice an opinion, but the elites use the Government to make all the decisions without asking the public. When the time comes, the elites will reduce the population without asking. We may not be around, but would you trust a politician or someone like Bill Gates to represent your vote on the future of your children? Wouldn't you like your grandchildren to have a voice on this issue?

When the founders wrote the Constitution and defined government organizations, like the Supreme Court, their purposes were noble, but time has counterfeited the social structures and the elites are ethnically biased.

The oligarchs bonded for power, and they used assassins to achieve their goals. As a result, the public has become a group of non-thinkers. Their platform to voice opinions has been destroyed. In the face of the television and the Internet, newspaper editorials are ignored. People no longer read. Society no longer functions as a unit.

There is a viral documentary titled *The Social Dilemma* describing how the tech giants manipulate the public. Former social media managers discussed the ramifications of biased Google and Facebook software systems. They sum up the enormous threat of social media. To make this worse, a single politician has no power to resolve this issue.

Control of society shouldn't be by monster Internet firms and the mafias, but if the U.S. shut down these organizations, other groups controlled by the same oligarchs would come along and more artfully game the system. It's all about greed.

The chapter titled *America's Washington Coup* brought out the possibility that the CIA now controls the mafias. Congress should investigate this possibility and take whatever action is necessary to make society manageable again.

Don't feel sorry for young voters. It's better to learn at a young age than to waste time on a crooked political system. Society can't let a bunch of uneducated, lower-class people run a country.

Rule 15: Develop your social skills. Seek truth and cast a wary eye. Avoid openly confronting the elites. Examine your surrounding social structure to join the winners. Join the political party that can benefit you the most, but in your mind stay independent and decide what your interests are.

Politics and Media

At the State Fair of Texas in Dallas in 1910, a half-white Indian chief saw the two-party game. Chief Quanah Parker spoke. "See my two hands. Here is one Indian way and one white way. Here is Republican Party and here is Democratic Party. I watch the two parties close. Which is the best?"

"The Democratic Party is trying to work for the good of all of us. It looks at rich and poor man same. Republican Party looks at rich man, but not good of poor man. This is why times are hard." [Y43]

The two-party political structure started long before Chief Parker. There are infinite ways to view two-party politics, and it requires logical thinking for a person to escape being committed to a party.

An average citizen isn't strong enough mentally to separate himself from the game. When a person is accepted by either party, his peers embrace him and he becomes part of what seems to be an intelligent movement.

The WASP-Jewish oligarchs in England fostered the development of a two-party political system - one party for the "conservatives" and the other referred to as the "liberals". Secretly both parties were controlled by Cecil Rhodes' group. Rhodes made sure his supporters occupied the major positions of power.

In the United States, the conservatives maintain control by holding the Constitution and the makeup of the Supreme Court static. They can't be taken to task because they are so strong society gives them a pass.

The Democrats collude also, but they're a band of losers. It wasn't always that way. Jack Kennedy and Lyndon Johnson were strong leaders. Things changed when Lyndon Johnson had the Democrats focus on integration.

Democrats claim to support diversity and the lower classes. They use contentious issues like abortion and gun control to polarize the public. Like the Republicans, they also use racism to hold their group together.

Money and name recognition are part of the game! Trump, Bloomberg, or Cuban have been depicted as intellectual businessmen. They are granted the option of running as a Republican or a Democrat because they are billionaires.

Dwight Eisenhower also could have run on either ticket with the image of a great military leader. Powerful wealthy candidates and celebrities with strong personalities have flexibility because there are no parties; there is a class. When the elites come into money and fame, they bond with other elites at a level where the thirst for money is sublimated by a thirst for power.

The U.S. has been built on the concept of socialism for the rich ever since FDR and WW II. Carroll Quigley correctly defined the Democrats as the "party of the fringes". [Y44]

Democrats represented whatever the GOP failed to select, and the GOP used to select all it needed to keep the game in its favor. The GOP rebalances as required. To disguise control, the presidency is rotated.

The media avoids conflict by never discussing the elites or important issues. Broadcasters like Rush Limbaugh and Sean Hannity never compete with any comparable talk-radio hosts. There can't be a debate on real issues because the sheep will wiggle away if they were asked to take a position. It's to the benefit of the media to offer dribble.

In Texas, the oil elite were part of the equation because crude oil became a requirement as part of the Grand Area strategy. The conservative white Christians in the Permian Basin in West Texas added to an already solid GOP base.

Around Fayetteville, the Austin Colonies were settled by white Europeans. Around 2010, the GOP realized how they could improve their position. They held a majority and they asked their voters to vote straight Republican. As the word got out, the Democratic incumbents switched parties; they ran as Republicans.

Along with gerrymandering and the white, Christian population in Texas, the state of Texas became a Republican stronghold, except for the major cities. Credit the GOP takeover in Texas to the oilmen and the conservative religious groups. They taught the sheep to pull the straight Republican lever.

The line between the two major parties is blurred. Neither political party considers average Americans and democracy. Republicans are no longer aligned with fiscal responsibility. Conservative elites ignore the budget. The GOP has decided to flush the U.S. dollar. It's a Jewish-Catholic game!

Except for Libertarians, all parties endorse an ever-increasing military budget, and they will permit military intervention anywhere. Bring on the drones. The good thing about that is perhaps we can keep our guns.

In the nineteenth and twentieth centuries, New York was the financial and commercial center of the United States. Since before the days of Teddy Roosevelt, the Tammany Hall group has been at the center of New York politics. They included immigrants, many of which were Jewish and Italian.

Because of J. Edgar Hoover's avoidance of the mafias, the Jewish and Italian clans controlled New York politics, and thus the Democratic Party. In the 1950s-1980s, New York generally had a Jewish mayor and then an Italian mayor, or vice-versa, but in the last forty years, the pattern changed. Jewish immigration increased. In 1989, a record number of Jews - more than seventy thousand - left the Soviet Union, mostly for the United States. [Y45] Many of them went to New York.

The Jewish group brought African Americans under their wing because they needed more political influence and inexpensive labor they could control, especially in the entertainment industry.

The previous New York governors were Spitzer, Paterson, and Cuomo - a Jewish person, an African American, and an Italian. Similarly, the previous New York mayors were Koch, Dinkins, Giuliani, Bloomberg, and de Blasio - two Italians, an African American, and two Jewish people.

Bill de Blasio, an Italian, was probably elected mayor of New York because he is married to an African American lady. To keep their seat at the elites' table, the Italians needed to gracefully wrest control from the Jewish Syndicate.

The collusion of the Jewish, Italian, and African American clans in NY allowed the Jewish elites to control the Democratic Party, entertainment, media, and the financial markets. The U.S. situation is similar to what occurred in Germany between WW I and WW II, where the Jewish people took control of publishing, banking, cinema, the stock market, the metals industry, professorships, and the arts.

Hillary Clinton appeared to control the Democratic National Committee [DNC], but the Jewish Syndicate pulled the strings. I was in Santa Fe and a prominent Jewish art gallery owner told me a story about a lady waiting in a line in Israel. This lady chatted with the person behind her in line. He told her he was part of a group working on developing candidates for the U.S. presidency. Hillary had not yet been elected to the Senate for the state of New York, but he said they were working with her and hoped she would win and might next become a presidential candidate.

In 2016, Debbie Wasserman Schultz ran the DNC, and NY Mayor Michael Bloomberg appeared on stage to encourage voters to support Hillary.

The Jewish Syndicate hedged their bet by helping Donald Trump and the Republican Party. With a little influence from the elite groups, the voters went along. Control of the United States was a bargain.

The oligarchs' Deep State has forced the public to elect a president whose goals are to seek personal gains. No recent presidential candidate has had the intellect to envision improving society and a backbone strong enough to create a more vibrant middle-class. The public has no chance to vote for a strong leader. The presidential candidates are only concerned with the control of voters and money.

In 2016, Trump had white voters supporting him who lived in different areas of town. One was a lower-class red-neck who was anti-black, anti-female, and/or anti-foreigner. Other support came from suburban elites, the white, status-quo seekers - Republican Christians. There were several other groups, such as sharp, racists who had been very successful; then there was the CIA and the other mafias.

In August 2020, I was wondering when the public would receive their second stimulus payment. At the time, Democratic Senator Nancy Pelosi explained that this legislation was so difficult it might take a week to resolve the issues.

Then on August 5, Democratic Senator Kamala Harris of California was interviewed and she explained her support for a new part of the bill to help fund small firms in the arts industry. Because she was a leading candidate for the Vice Presidential position, the Democrats had chosen to give her media time.

At the same time, Texas Republican Senator John Cronyn, Mitch McConnell's favorite brown-nose, was also supportive of the arts sponsorship Kamala was backing. The Republicans didn't want to be left out.

The next day, New York Democratic Senator Chuck Schumer further explained why it was so difficult to get both sides to agree on the bill to give the voters trillions of dollars. Schumer's explanation was a lie. Both parties were playing politics. They were blocking a second stimulus payment.

The one thing voters agree on is that they should vote out of office 95% of Congressmen. It is probably higher than that. About the only GOP senators that should remain are Romney and Sassi. The politicians are liars and a waste of time. Term limits are necessary.

When Trump was elected, the wealthy were the first to receive tax breaks; next, the military's budget was increased. The mafias were subsequently favored with a DOJ ruling on gambling. That ruling helped reinforce online poker as gambling and sports betting as not gambling. How about that for a lie?

The Catholics got two Supreme Court members, the Attorney General, and the President. The Israelis got everything they could hope for, and when Covid-19 appeared the wealthy were thrown trillions of dollars.

No Jewish lawyer, doctor, or filmmaker in the United States will make any statement opposed to the Israelis. The Israelis are a tight, clannish group. They teach their children to act as if they're superior. That's ultimate racism, worse than the KKK.

The Jewish group is bonded to the CIA and mafias, as are other clans. This gives them enormous power because their lawyers have gained control of the financial system.

The oligarchs believe they have bought a ticket to the future. In reality, now should be the time to "change the sheets" so future generations won't be forced to listen to the whisper of the elites' pawns.

To change our social structure, the public must understand how the elites control them. The conservatives are the winners, the chosen ones. Rush Limbaugh harped on this concept when he described Republicans as a party of the winners. The Republicans are the winners because the GOP has the support of the two most successful power groups - the religious groups [with their mafias] and the military.

The remaining masses are an adversarial group they refer to as liberals or socialists. Carroll Quigley defined the Democratic Party as the *fringes*, which is a polite definition for losers.

The leaders of the conservative and liberal Deep State workers are trained to lead the sheep down a path where the oligarchs have total control. The oligarchs' pawns can whisper in the sheep's' ears and tell them what they want them to believe. That's the case now and their influence is more than a whisper. They use Facebook and YouTube to bias the masses. This "play" is well into the final act.

The masses keep their heads down and accept fake news. The media takes advantage of this inability of the sedimentary and the non-thinkers. There is no debate on issues, only regurgitation of biased news. The sheep are trying to survive. They can't think about anything but their next paycheck.

There are many highly-intelligent sheep. I had a friend who was a graduate of a prestigious high school and a prestigious college. He became a large hospital administrator. He was 100% politically correct. He never took a risky position, and he did popular things, like playing music. As an extrovert, he was always in demand to entertain the flock.

Businesswise, my friend was tremendously talented. Like former Secretary of Defense Robert Gates, my friend knew how to evaluate and administrate. Put Barack Obama and Robert Gates in the sheep tank; being a sheep is not a negative.

As an example of this herding of the sheeple, one of Churchill's famous quotes implied a person should be liberal by the age of 20, but he would be stupid if by age 40 he wasn't a conservative.

Churchill was playing a game his hero Cecil Rhodes developed. Churchill took a racist-cultist stance to be the leader of the Conservative Party in England. Churchill was a great leader, but he was also a Deep State conservative and an extraordinary schemer.

Churchill's game has been extended in the U.S. In early 2020, Sean Hannity offered Churchill's famous quote as an example of conservatism. Churchill's quote sounds perfect, but it is just rhetoric used by the GOP media to sell the conservative cause and disadvantage the public. Hannity set the stage for the GOP's politicians. The media leaders are the heroes, and they are expected to be the greatest storytellers and liars. They are the spokespeople with the gall and wit to hide the elite's schemes and pretend to help the sheeple.

The GOP creates a problem and then they have the media complain that voters are being taken advantage of by "liberals." For instance, the GOP maintained the welfare system for decades. The GOP doesn't solve welfare issues. They could, but the only solution the GOP elites find appealing is something like reducing social security.

The GOP elites have exasperated the welfare problem because they needed a focal point to target their adversary. The GOP sheep have learned to smile as the lies are told. Some are naïve and they act like a joke was said. They think they have joined the white-man's club.

Rush Limbaugh understood. He contended the Democratic leaders focus on losers and talk down to their sheep. The leaders of the Democratic Party talk down to their sheep.

It would help if someone would bring the masses together and clear the air so there could be a discussion of real issues.

When you have a biased speaker like Rush Limbaugh, there will be no impartial discussions on major issues. That's why Geraldo Rivera got on Limbaugh's case for spewing irresponsible rhetoric after the GOP had their case rejected by the Supreme Court.

Rule 16: There should be a scale for media facilitators to be judged, but as long as the elites are in control, there

will be no honest media. You may have to read a few great books
each year to get the facts.

Unions

Where dad grew up in Oklahoma, there was a lot of oil activity, so he was always interested in oilmen and leasing properties. He cultivated several relationships with lease hounds and oilmen. He invited E.E. Townes, who was part of the founders' group of Humble Oil & Refining Company, to come quail hunting. [I'll assume Townes was Jewish.]

Townes had his chauffeur drive him to Fayetteville and they would bring two bird dogs. Maybe a couple of other hunters would participate. Dad would ask perhaps 40 or 50 landowners if they could hunt their properties so they would have larger acreage to hunt.

Hunting wasn't about shooting Bob White quail. It was wonderful to be part of nature and watch beautiful birddogs work.

The hunters would shoot a few quail and the chauffeur would clean them. It was about having a conversation on the subjects of oil, unions, politics, and the world; and being in the great outdoors, or about taking a break for lunch and eating barbecue brisket and sausage at the Prause Meat Market in LaGrange.

Oilmen hate unions; they love to break them. Townes espoused John L. Lewis was doing a terrible thing by having his coal miners' strike to get more money for the union workers.

Dad countered by saying, "You should applaud Lewis's efforts. If he gets more money for them, the price of coal goes up, and you get to sell your crude for more money."

Few conservative oilmen argue against making more money.

I've had several instances where I had interplay with unions. I was in Dallas with a computer company [NCS Computing] and we won a contract with Jaggars-Chiles-Stovall Co., a photographic and printing company, to typeset the Dallas-Ft.

Worth phone directories. JCS was a union shop. We teamed up with them to take the bid away from a non-union shop. [Lee Harvey Oswald had once worked for JCS.]

Later, I manage a contract team for Mustang in Houston, a large Caterpillar dealership. Our contractors programmed to maintain a safety stock in the inventory. Caterpillar paid dealerships the going rate of interest, about seven percent at the time, to warehouse a six-months supply of parts. When the union struck, the workers were unable to affect Caterpillar's operation for six months. That gave Caterpillar the leverage to write a better contract with the union.

Software development people were usually non-union. I asked dad, "Why are unions required?"

He said, "If I were not a union member, my boss could tell me, 'See those boxes on that train car. Put one of those in the back of my pickup.' If I didn't, he could fire me."

I am not sure I bought dad's argument, but I saw several situations where unions were broken by big corporations with sophisticated computer systems. The equation gets changed in favor of the big employer when computers gain enough control of the operations.

I was in Seattle when Boeing forced their workers to grandfather benefits and wages, effectively selling out the next generation of workers.

The problem with unions is the Mafia or Israeli clan use organizers to control the unions. For instance, the Jewish Syndicate controls service workers, the teachers, and the movie industry. The Israelis use unions to gain political clout.

In 2005, the Service Workers International Union [SEIU] is controlled by the Jewish Syndicate. In 2005 they and the Teamsters bolted the AFL-CIO and set up separate Unions.

The Teamsters were regarded as a union run by the Mafia. The SEIU's president from 1996 to 2010 was Andy Stern; Stern is considered a Jewish name.

The SEIU had approximately 1.9 million workers in the U.S. and Canada. They spent $28M on Obama's 2008 presidential campaign, part of which they raised for Obama. Hundreds of thousands of SEIU members organized rallies and voted.

I went to a rally in the small town of Flatonia, Texas in Fayette County. Fayette County is GOP territory, but the SEIU was there to bring out the voters at Robert's Steakhouse.

In 2012, the SEIU helped Obama return to office, reporting almost $70M in support. In 2016, the SEIU again pledged $70M to support Hillary Clinton and Democratic Senate candidates. After Trump's victory, the SEIU cut their budget by 30%.

The Jewish Syndicate also influences the teacher's union. In 2019, Randi Weingarten, the gay Jewish leader of the Federation of Teachers, took a verbal swipe at Kamala Harris, a candidate she would normally support. Why would a NY Jewish union leader try to hurt the campaign of an African American?

Ms. Weingarten seems to have been trying to help position Joe Biden. Was Miss Weingarten part of a GOP scheme to elevate the weaker candidate, memory-impaired Joe Biden? Was this to push down the campaign of Bernie Sanders and help Trump?

Unions are a tool of the Israeli and the Italian mafias. They are used to control money and votes.

For decades the Jewish Syndicate controlled the actors and actresses. This allowed the Jewish elite to control the distribution of movies. This control allowed Lyndon Johnson and the military to succeed in the JFK assassination.

A previous chapter discussed how Lyndon Johnson's man in Hollywood, Jack Valenti, was "promoted" by LBJ to be president of the Academy of Motion Picture Arts and Sciences. One of Johnson's Jewish sponsors, Lew Wasserman, met weekly with Valenti and other AMPAS lawyers and producers. For four decades, the titans of the movie industry protected LBJ.

The AMPAS was a union designed to control the movie industry. It is run by Jews. They did not produce factual movies. They implied they produced entertainment, but it was a biased Jewish monopoly. If any union needs to be reorganized, it is the union run by AMPAS. They are one reason conspiracies persist.

Rule 17: Visualize the elites' organizations and how they function. If you can, help counter the unions controlled by oligarchs or political groups. That may include AMPAS, SEIU, the teacher's union, and the Teamsters. [Self-driving trucks may be the end of the Teamsters.]

Entrepreneurship

The oligarchs control technology because it's valuable. Intellectual property and knowledge represent power. The oligarchs have pawns kill for intellectual property. It's capitalism at its finest.

Recently, one person was the only survivor in a large cancer study. His doctor was floored when the patient acknowledged he had taken one drug that was not part of the study.

The hospital running the tests had a few years earlier canceled a study with the drug he had taken because they were not going to be able to patent any of the results; therefore, they wouldn't be able to control the profits if their tests were successful.

I was once the fourth person in a four-man English company named Elliot Automation. I can't remember if Elliot had one "l" or two.

After a few months, the Elliots offered me 10% of their company, which I declined for the wrong reasons. They were wonderful people. Typically, the English loved beer, darts, and camaraderie. They were light-hearted and easy to work for. Being a small company, if you were working past five, it was fine to make a beer run.

Elliot Automation developed process control systems primarily for oil companies. The president and senior, Peter Elliot, marketed the systems and his brother designed and built the hardware. The systems were of industrial quality and state-of-the-art. They featured optically isolated ports. Low power requirements allowed them to run off small NiCad batteries.

One system I wrote the software for controlled turbines, which converted geothermal energy into electricity. The system had dual processors for automatic backup. Shell was our client. One day, Peter Elliot, his brother, and I went to the Shell building in Houston. We met with Shell's lead technical guy on the project. He was an expert on analog. Analog is kind of like a wave, a voltage flow.

The Shell expert brought his flowchart overview of the system, and we brought ours. All we had basically was a rectangle representing software logic with input and output ports going into the bottom of the rectangle. It looked like a rectangular centipede without a head.

Their analog guy brought a big drawing that showed dozens of interconnected analog chips to represent his hardware solution. I had never done analog systems, so I had no clue what he had designed. It was just a bunch of inflexible hardware connected in a particular sequence.

What we had was scalable. We could add more memory and another input or output.

Our system could read an input in yards or meters or joules or Fahrenheit. When the reading came in through one of the optically isolated ports, the binary number would be four digits or greater and calibrated on a scale for the input device - an exact measurement representing a percentage of the range.

If we shipped the system to people who understood yards instead of meters, when I output the reading to display, I'd convert the percentage to yards before the system displayed it. This complete flexibility was like having liquid hardware.

When we left the Shell meeting, I had to ask, "What did he show us?" Then we all laughed about it.

Why would a small company like Elliot Automation be awarded a contract by a monster corporation like Shell? Of course, the Elliots were connected and very conservative. They brought pro-life concepts with them. They taught conservatism wherever they went.

The English set the standard for conservatism, and now the English are doing a wicked good job with entrepreneurship. Richard Branson in his book, *Finding My Virginity*, sells the leadership of Barack Obama, Nelson Mandela, Desman Tutu, and

David Cameron. Branson sprinkles in entrepreneurs, the likes of Elon Musk, Larry Page, and Jeff Bezos.

Branson speculates the U.S. could use an entrepreneurial president, but not necessarily a technical one like Elon Musk, possibly just a pure entrepreneur like himself. One may think of someone like Mark Cuban. Cuban knows technology, especially software. He could be a strong candidate.

The world doesn't need an entrepreneur like Branson. Branson spews self-serving elitism. He believes he correctly shapes the world as he spins England's golden decoy of entrepreneurship.

Branson selects good people and sets up great new businesses. A large percentage of the time Branson will later be forced to sell out those employees and take his millions when he can't press through the other elites' walls. But Branson appears to do the pure thing. He gives young, aggressive people the opportunity to push aside some of those older folks that had worked for 20 years for earlier entrepreneurial companies.

Most importantly for England, Branson gives young people a cause to follow - entrepreneurship. The elites use politicians and entrepreneurs as a front. They dangle the bait out there, like monetary contests to get into space or entrepreneurial TV shows. "Yes, let's sponsor space trips for wealthy people. We'll use the same cargo bays to drop our laser weapons into space. We'll get Musk or Branson or Bezos to bid on it. That will get the young people excited. We can't just play the adversarial game all the time."

The English invented elitism and mastered how to elevate politicians. The English use the equity markets to control venture investments, and they present rare individual successes as a symbol to convey hope for their masses.

Richard Branson, a minted decoy like Cecil Rhodes, provides hope for the English to retain the use of some of the power of a sovereign currency. Branson, a sophisticated entrepreneur, has access to English secrets, and his Virgin

Galactic space-race involvement shows creativity. Branson is glorified because the English elites have to try to control technology. The elites use technocrats as bait when entrepreneurs like Branson herd the sheep by selling them socialism under the guise of opportunity.

Recently Branson has had a turn in luck and the English government doesn't seem as helpful. They seem to think Branson hasn't paid enough taxes. Of course, the U.S. Branson is Elon Musk.

Entrepreneurs funded by taxpayers are much more exciting than politicians and soldiers, but if that fails, then it's ale at the pub or their form of football - soccer.

English and U.S. universities and colleges are an extension of technocrats and entrepreneurs. Higher education institutions provide a mechanism to educate young people, and a methodology to keep people chasing their dream.

Sports - football, basketball, baseball - fit into this category providing more intellectual stimulus and excitement. Like the concept of life after death, young people need a purpose in life, a concept to pursue that's exciting.

Years ago, I asked a Kuwait sheik what he invested in. He and his brother had bought a couple of service stations. I couldn't see his investments as motivating.

People are fortunate to have exciting games, celebrities, educational opportunities, and the chance to borrow money and repay it over a working lifetime. The CEOs of major banks are thankful for our elitist systems.

Imagine, if the next generation does everything correctly, instead of playing the role of sycophants for the elites, technology could allow the masses to work intelligently and escape the big city. Only 50% of the work would be required. Yes, dream on!

Rule 18: Be a technocrat and embrace entrepreneurship. That will be hard because the world needs fewer people. Perhaps

no one needs to get killed if we are logical and the oligarchs
learn to share.   Those are two big ifs.

Bureaucracy

"When you see that in order to produce, you need to obtain permission from men who produce nothing ... when you see that money is flowing to those who deal not in goods, but in favors ... when you see that men get richer by graft and pull more than by work, and your laws don't protect you against them, but protect them against you ... when you see corruption being rewarded and honesty becoming a self-sacrifice ... you may know that society is doomed." Ayn Rand

Ms. Rand wrote slightly before large multinational corporations began to dominate the world - before computer databases allowed big corporations to control information.

Corporations are an overpowering force. They organize skilled teams to complete complex projects. Like a feeding machine, the continuous improvement of computer technology allows corporations to dominate international business. Every month development teams improve processes. If they implement inferior technology, they are pushed aside by competitors.

Huge corporate budgets feed projects to improve processes and develop new products. Complex products are hard to successfully release because they may have undiscovered problems. For instance, in the 1960s IBM released a large operating system they referred to as OS. OS had millions of lines of code, and the initial release had thousands of software errors.

A friend of mine met with an OS developer in Endicott, NY. He asked the developer about the criteria for new OS releases. Over a few beers, the response was, "When we get the number of known errors to less than a thousand, then we do a new release."

Each subsequent release of OS cured hundreds of problems, but like a big storm uncovering shells on the beach, new problems would appear. It took years for IBM to get control of their big operating system.

As technology and conditions change, products also need to change. When innovative advancements are possible, they need to be integrated into products. If corporations don't improve concepts, rules, or policies as things change, the system can become too difficult to sustain. The system may become unwieldy.

I worked on a computer system for heavy equipment distributors. We handled the inventories which consisted of parts from all the equipment manufacturers. Each piece of equipment or part had a number of categories - part number, description, unit type, number of units, replacement part number, quantity, size, weight, etc.

A small vendor might have 15 categories whereas a large vendor, like Caterpillar, might have 45 categories. Of all the equipment vendors we handled, Allis Chalmers probably had the greatest number of categories, and they had the hardest time keeping their specifications current.

It didn't surprise me when Allis Chalmers declared bankruptcy. Their management may have over-engineered their products. They failed to simplify their system, and that may have allowed their workers to attain job security, but they fell on their sword.

Congress passes more complex legislation each year designed to give the elites' more control. Financial legislation is an example. The 1913 Federal Reserve Act had 31 pages. The 1933 Glass-Steagall Act only had 37 pages. In 1994 the Interstate Banking Efficiency Act had 61 pages. The 1999 Gramm-Leach-Bliley Act had 145 pages, but the 2010 Dodd-Frank bill went over the top with 2,319 pages.

Health care legislation is another example. Medicare, Medicaid, and Obamacare were too big and complex. When White House sources said that the Obamacare software had 600 known errors, I was sure their estimate was low. It would have taken years to properly fix the Obamacare software problems, and when an organization has to focus on maintenance, there is no time for real improvement.

Government agencies generally have less incentive to become more efficient. Unlike an Allis Chalmers, the failure of a government agency seldom occurs because the government can add more funds. A government agency may make problems larger and more complex so it can add staff and raise salaries.

The public should be thankful the Internet is a competitive force helping to clean up government inefficiencies. The cell-phone has been an enormous help. Counter to that, it seems to be more difficult to get responsible government people on the line so you can ask simple questions. Government agencies assume the computer will handle the questions and customer service isn't required. The public is not viewed as a customer.

In 2013, at a Super Bowl gathering in Biloxi, I talked with Bea Harrison who owned the Encore Group. Bea regularly put on TV shows that were mostly documentaries where she interviewed local business leaders. Those establishments paid Bea for the interview, which was a form of advertising for them.

Bea had her firm for about 25 years and was grandfathered into FOX where she could buy time on the FOX network. One day FOX told her that because of the new legislation in the Dodd-Frank bill she would have to add closed-captioning to her broadcasts. Bea could not afford to do that, but big networks like ABC, CBS, NBC, and FOX could afford the new requirements.

One of the major networks offered Bea a job. She declined, saying, "I can't. I've never worked for anyone [and I won't start now]." Perhaps she has reconsidered.

Small production companies should not have been required to have closed-captioning. Of course, it's too late for firms that had production rights to have their rights revalidated. Unfortunately, no political party protects the middle-class or small companies, and bad legislation is never rewritten.

The shutting down of small media producers is an example of where big businesses got the government to pass laws that would eliminate small business owners. The elites used their corporations to pressure political parties to pass favorable legislation. Elites can afford to have legislation written for them. Money and complexity work for larger firms.

The President, Congressmen, and lobbyists helped the elites' corporations gain favorable tax treatment and eliminate smaller competition under the guise of protecting the public.

Like Ayn Rand, Marx and Engel wrote their theories before the world was dominated by multi-national corporations with large databases.

I see only one difference between the U.S. corporate management and communist management. Both have the same incentives and in both cases the president must appease the big investor or donor.

Government divisions and agencies always are dominated by politics. Corporations reflect the opinions of the oligarchs that own the controlling stock, and therefore the Allied oligarchs must control the president of the United States just like they control a corporate president. There is no such thing as democracy in politics.

In my two prior books, I wrote paragraphs on Daniel J. Hennessy. In the chapter *The Texans* in *JFK and the World Oligarchy*, I wrote that Buster or Danny had tremendous contacts and I implied that he may have flown Carlos Marcello back to the United States after Bobby had Marcello thrown out of the country.

In *2020 – The Year of the New World Order* I also wrote that Buster confided in me, "The military is a huge uncontrollable entity. The politics are horrendous. If you put someone in a position within the military and try to control any part of the military, they may turn on you and destroy you. All you can do is control the man on top."

This defines the basic difference between the military and a division in a corporation. Therefore, Marx and Engel were totally wrong because they could not envision a computerized society. The major nations will eventually gravitate to the same form of social structures.

Rule 19: Bureaucracy is an incubator of socialism, a consequence of population growth and elitism. Ignore bureaucracy.

Government is like a corporation controlled by oligarchs. Focus on improving processes and legislation.

Structural Evolution

The peak traffic in poker rooms is the day after Thanksgiving. After Thanksgiving the public's view turns to the holidays; it becomes time to put up a tree with lights and ornaments and spend money.

In the 1990s, the peak of L.L. Bean's mail-order operation to 20M customers was also near the Thanksgiving holidays. Bean had a lady managing the temporaries brought in for the Christmas rush. The staff making a presentation to her commented that her mind was single-threaded. If more than one new concept was presented in a meeting it would confuse her. Of course, it is to the company's advantage that she was laser-focused while managing thousands of employees.

Today's society is also single-tracked. In many cases, a significant amount of critical knowledge is required. Technology combined with a complex social structure can create a situation with detrimental effects. It takes one Lehman Brothers or a miss-programmed jetliner to gum up the works.

Major events can be a horrific injustice, but often it's hard to evaluate whether those changes were for better or worse. Most major events are not repeatable. They may be like a 2,000-year flood, and because of the complexity of the personalities and society, no one can agree. We wind up having many different opinions.

Abrupt changes are generally caused by a weakness in our financial or social structures. When strong groups and an extraordinary event come together, society realigns behind the winners. The result can be wonderful for a large segment of society. As an example, Churchill and Roosevelt used the conclusion of the war in 1945 to reshape society and history. Their realignment worked splendidly until 1971 when the gold standard was changed and the elite began searching for inexpensive foreign labor.

By the 1980s, after the CIA established media control, television was the primary media form. In 1989 at a Whole Earth Festival at the University of California, Timothy Leary saw it coming when he said, "Television is everything. You know that. Who controls television controls the minds of people? ... Get yourself in front of a TV camera and you're going to change things." [Y46]

Beginning in 2000, the Internet increasingly usurped the power of television, newspapers, and books. Software and communications created a virtual world, which cell phones and personal computers extended. The CIA then began to capture all cell-phone and Internet content.

The elites use their static systems to stonewall the masses. This erroneous definition allows the elites to enrich themselves. As long as the elites control the presidency and SCOTUS, they will continue to limit the Constitution and the Supreme Court, and our Government will remain biased.

Boeing is an example of how critical software technology has become. For years planes had specific systems that were generally programmed to do a minimum number of tasks. Much of the thinking was left to the pilots. If birds took out an engine, the pilots would over-ride the system and land the big beast in the river.

The size of the plane and the scope of the computer functionality grew and grew and grew. Finally, one day the software design team decided the huge plane was too complex for the pilots to handle all of the critical decisions. The computer could decide from digital feedback if birds had taken out an engine. Rather than waiting 60 seconds for a pilot to decide what had happened, the plane's computer software could immediately take corrective action.

If the software system took over the additional functionality, then the flight crew could be reduced by a person. They could use a six-man crew rather than a seven-man crew. In fact, they could have the computer take over a few more functions so the pilots could relax more and think less. Then, wow, they could use a five-man crew and even have one pilot as kind of as a backup person. Of course, this is all a guess on my part. I wasn't there.

I did a contract software job in Everett, Washington, which is up Highway 5 just north of Seattle. For a public electrical utility, our group converted their system from the IBM disk operating system to IBM's large operating system, from DOS to OS.

Each day I would drive by Boeing. Boeing was unionized, and since my dad was a union member and my software work was non-union, I had a keen interest in what the Boeing management did to break their union.

The union struck around September. As Thanksgiving approached, the large Boeing parking area started to have more cars parking each day. The workers were being forced by their wives to break the union lines because the families couldn't survive the Christmas season without a paycheck. It wasn't long before the union caved and took the solution of grandfathering the older union employees.

I believe the Boeing plane problems were caused because the software controlling planes had got much bigger and the software guys were treated like janitors, necessary people, but people who it was okay to ignore.

The engineers designing the planes, the brilliant "skunk-works" types that won the big contracts, they were the important employees, or at least that was the perception. The upper management, which may include some outside the corporation hedge-fund types, thought they couldn't possibly pay some stupid programmer hundreds of thousands of dollars, on a scale with the other brilliant engineers. I mean, "We're talking software!"

And when the big monster plane fishtails into the earth the financial studs running Boeing still don't get it. They can't realize the software is beyond the scope of their under-paid and under-intelligent union staff. They can't visualize that they need to find great software engineers to solve this problem. This is like a corporation has taken a hundred construction people who built houses and asked them to build a hundred story building. How would that work?

It's not like there was one problem with the software where if you fixed that then everything will run properly. Maybe there were five different problems, and if you fix one the others can still take the plane down.

The software was never designed perfectly. Something was wrong with its functionality because it was pieced together over time. When you add additional functions to a system the flaws become apparent. You can't solve the problems by only solving one problem and the problems don't show up in routine tests.

The world's biggest companies have this problem when they drastically enhanced the functionality of their computer systems. In some cases, they brought in tremendous experts after the first failure. Those system engineers would solve one problem and another would show up after the experts left. That would go on for a year. Finally, corporate management would give up and have the equipment removed.

Our military has had similar problems as Boeing. They were accustomed to buying things like tanks that had limited capability. Now they will have robot tanks, and what do the generals know about integrated software. Nothing! They'll give an enormous sum of money to a big-name corporation so they will look good, but they won't hire and pay some expert what he would be worth to solve software problems.

The generals aren't able to talk intelligently with a software person. That's because military executives don't come up through the software ranks. The generals are the hierarchical leaders. How could they possibly pay someone a fair wage when the software worker isn't a lawyer or politician or military mind? That's the mentality.

Donald Trump and the Congressmen had no idea what they were doing. The general public was worse. Because someone made a few million dollars in construction and oil and raising cattle, that made him think he knew something.

Successful business leaders, who are worth millions, know they're right 99.7% of the time. They know about hammers, nails, concrete, oil, real estate, and accounting. Their experience tells them that construction projects are like software projects – they generally take longer and cost more than projected. Their solution is to fire or sue someone if a project has problems. They write long, detailed contracts so they can sue if the project fails.

I talked with a successful rural cowboy. He was a 100% Trump supporter. I listened to him and replied, "I couldn't vote for Hillary either." I didn't tell him I didn't vote for Trump either because he was so sure.

I gave him a hint of what I concluded: "When Trump got elected, he increased the military budget and reduced taxes. That was what Ronald Reagan did, and Reagan proved doing those two things cause a big deficit. It's obvious, the Trump administration will run a deficit of over a trillion dollars a year."

This successful businessman *immediately* told me how great Trump was. It would have been a waste of time for me to try to influence his opinions. Anything I might say would be ignored. He was self-made and experienced, and he ignored my spot-on point.

That's the ultimate sedimentary memory. I had tried to be subtle, but *immediately* he told me he had the *only* valid perspective, that the GOP spin was the Bible. To him, everything Trump and the GOP did was right, and the Democrats were a left-wing group that should be eliminated. This person has a high IQ, but he loved his opinions because he strenuously repeated his assessment. I didn't mind! Warren Buffett was right; you can always tell someone he's wrong tomorrow. That lesson took me a long time to learn.

Our government has had this Grand Area plan to control the world and both apples and oranges are supporting our grand military. People are asked to choose whether they want to be an apple in the 53% GOP conservative monopoly or be an underdog in the 47% Democratic orange category.

The first problem is that we have incompetent leaders because technology in the last 20 years has changed. By the time the executives arrive, their thinking is obsolete. They don't understand the digital world of software, databases, and communications.

Because of their lack of vision and society's restricted military-mafia-religion-ethnic clan environment, the only thing the elite leaders can control is loyalty. Loyalty was number one on Trump's list! His only solution was, "You're fired! Or, if you violate my non-disclosure agreement, I'll sue!"

I have had non-disclosure agreements. I got an offer from a pattern-recognition company in Silicon Valley. My prior employer, the firm whose major investor's father was Jesse Jones' only attorney, threatened to sue. The California people told me not to worry about it because NDAs aren't big in California. That sounded good, but since they were about to go public, they decided they couldn't risk the publicity.

Our political leaders are a contrast to leaders like Franklin Roosevelt or the French King Louis XIV.

Franklin Roosevelt very carefully selected his cabinet members. Although a Democrat, Roosevelt had no qualms appointing Republicans to his cabinet if they were the best qualified.

Louis XIV wrote his grandson when his grandson was leaving to become king of Spain: "Never favor those who flatter you the most, but hold rather to those who risk your displeasure for your own good. Never neglect business for pleasure … Make every effort to know men of distinction so you may call on them when you need them. Be courteous to all, speak hurtful to no man." [Y47]

There wasn't any WW I or WW II software technology, but today we have a flaw in our system because technology is too complex and the politicians are not equipped to deal with it. Neither are lawyers and college professors. Musk and a few others are, but they don't have time for this.

Any Boeing type problems will be fixed. The right people will eventually be paid enough to fix the problems. A company like Boeing has too much money at risk.

Afterward, the system will remain static for a long period. The brilliant engineers will get bored and leave to pursue more challenging problems. Years later, other people will come along and have new challenges.

We trust our issues to our elites and their pawns, but this is uncharted territory. The elites could make a change and one mistake could lead to another. The super-powers believe they are going to split the pie and squeeze the sheep. The problems are not new to them, but the sheep need to understand the elites are not special. As George Orwell wrote, "The average millionaire is just the average dishwasher dressed in a new suit."

After the international bankers met to discuss China, I was told about their meeting. A week or so later, Trump repeated exactly what they discussed in those meetings. If the President repeats what the international bankers say, then he is influenced by the banking oligarchs who stand behind their bankers.

Just notice how absurd the list of 2020 Democratic candidates was. It was a zoo. The Democrats had divided leadership and the GOP should have taken advantage of that, but Trump had a big mouth and threatened everyone, particularly people on social security and Medicare.

The United States needs leadership that is part of society, a non-political, non-control, non-racist part. The Jews, Catholics, and Muslims need to modify their storyline and get inclusive. They are not fooling as many people. The FB quote was: The next authoritarian needs to be more competent.

Because they are clannish, the Catholics and the Jewish members of the Supreme Court should be replaced. They and the Deep State mismanaged the world-order game.

Barack Obama was not totally effective, but he did advance the African American image and he had good intentions. Obama was hampered by racism. A racist, super-power leader like Putin wasn't going to sign any agreement with an African American or a lady like Hillary Clinton. Michelle Obama would have the same problems, regardless of her capabilities.

These problems go deeper. Our nation's biggest problem is our racist system. The United States has shown that they can't make correct big decisions because many of our problems are race-related.

In the 1990s, I was on a flight to Seattle. A large rice farmer and his wife, my relative, a Schramm, were on the same flight. I was doing a contract software job near Seattle and his wife had gone to college near Seattle. The Texas Aggies were about to play a great Washington Huskies football team. By coincidence, we were all going to see the game and I was going to continue working near Seattle.

My in-law mentioned he had an African American working for him who had just gotten a divorce. He told his employee, "I can't tell you how sorry I am to hear about your divorce."

The response he got was, "Oh, we still get together every evening. It just got where we were losing so much money because we were married. Everybody we associated with was laughing at us."

We haven't solved segregation, integration, or immigration. This problem has gotten bigger. We have built a social structure that traps people into a welfare system built around divorce or nefarious businesses. We have generated a cash society of unmarried women and smugglers.

The system is self-defeating. There's no escape. The women have a handful of children from different fathers and it would cost them too much in taxes and benefits to go to work and be part of society. If a person on welfare gets a legitimate job, their welfare cuts off and they have to pay taxes.

Our system has failed because there has been a major shift in our social mix and society has not integrated the new workers effectively. In 1950 non-whites were 10% of the U.S. population. By 2014 the percentage was 34%. [Y48]

The 24% increase in non-white workers overloaded the job market because the predominantly white society always gets the better paying jobs. When the unwed mother could make more money by not working, that ruined the non-white society. Female children were brought to believe that men need to pay for sex.

Just so we don't misunderstand each other, I am getting this from white men who date non-white women. Almost 100% of the time the non-white women expect money whereas with the white girls the requests are perhaps 10%. I could continue this analysis and give my explanation of the effects on young white girls and their relationship to non-white men, but just assume there are also resultant issues in that social mix.

Society rationalizes and thinks a few high-paid athletes will somehow make it all be right and come together. The politicians don't discuss this and solve it. They are not lazy; this subject is not a win-win for anyone.

These issues stem from society trying to make room for more people or the elites working to create groups of people they can more easily control. If this nation is to rise above the times and advance, it has to take on the more difficult issues and solve them in a professional manner. The issues need to be communicated to the public.

I've managed computer centers where I had sixty problems on my list. Many times, problems between 15 and 30 bypassed problems between 5 and 14. There were some very difficult problems in that high-middle range that would just take too long to fix.

I think the United States needs at least four presidents and they need to concentrate on resolving big issues and not passing laws for the rich. The issues can be compartmentalized as foreign affairs, domestic issues, social structure problems, and no-win issues.

As an example of a no-win issue, when someone loses a national race but wins the popular vote by a few million votes, "how does one audit electronic votes?" Why can't we do away with mail ballots and allow online voting. With the existing technology, we should easily be able to solve that problem. We should not allow this fiasco to continue.

Rule 20: Help correct society's social problems by providing non-political, non-biased voice to your peers. Above all, you must try to be an exception parent, and that implies talking to your children and understanding their issues.

Software Versus Hardware

The U.S. government is out of sync. The Grand Area plans, the Phoenix Program, SCOTUS, DOJ, the Constitution, and the two-party system are aged. The policies and structures designed for elite control were fine when they were created, but social structures need to breathe as the world advances.

As a personal example, there are problems with software patents. Software is too flexible for patent analysts to objectively separate the relative merits of the applicants' arguments. Software is not as contained as a piece of hardware, and this leads to overlap and conflict. Perhaps the rules for software patents should be different than hardware patents, and the importance of software patents should probably be prorated.

In the Alice Ruling, SCOTUS defined software was abstract, which is absurd. Software code may be inefficient, but software is never abstract. It is not like a subjective painting.

The Alice ruling implied hardware was superior to software. Nonsense! Software is a form of digital control and therefore flexible. All the members of SCOTUS that approved that should have been terminated.

This false definition of software took place for several reasons. First, a large amount of old elite money is tied to existing patented hardware devices. Second, SCOTUS was duped into support because Supreme Court members are illiterate when it comes to technology. Third, some SCOTUS members are tied to the elites. The Catholic and Jewish members support the Vatican and Israel. The Italian and Jewish mafias have long-standing Supreme Court connections, and our Allies need to protect their special interests.

With our controlled media, the U.S. social structure is kept static. The public has been taught the Supreme Court is filled with brilliant lawyers. False! The Supreme Court is loaded with non-technical lawyers who are incompetent. They are at the mercy of the Deep Stators. The Alice Ruling paralleled the English rules by declaring online software patents for games to be too abstract. The British were protecting their gambling revenues, and they influenced the U.S. Republicans.

It used to be that an individual could participate economically with patents, but now each country has upped the ante by placing their restrictions on the patent process. This change causes people to file patents in each nation or a group of nations, like the European Union.

This change is not to the individual's advantage. The elites can have their corporations spend a half-million dollars to submit a particular patent application in fifty countries. The money may be a grant from a government agency to the corporation. An individual can't afford to participate.

Software didn't exist when the Constitution was written. It was beyond the imagination of the writers of our Constitution. At the time, everything was analog, and not digital.

Software is like liquid hardware. It's certainly not abstract, and software patents should be far more significant than hardware patents because software is completely flexible and therefore more important. It eliminates a lot of hardware. Think of software as an email as compared to a letter as a representation of hardware.

Software patents should be more important than hardware patents, but the public and the Supreme Court are too mentally restricted [retarded] to formulate proper opinions. SCOTUS members are influenced by our Allied elites as is the Deep State.

The Alice ruling had to be influenced by the English. They established similar laws, and they are seeking to control online gambling in the Allied nations. Former colonies like India and Australia have fallen in step with them.

The George W. Bush administration may have had a lot to do with this because of the Bush's connection with the Carlyle Group included Tony Blair, Jim Baker, and the bin Ladens.

Because of international elite influence, an individual can no longer bear the expense of applying for patents in 50 nations that have different laws. The software patent system of each nation having different rules is too costly. It used to be different. One relatively inexpensive international patent was all that was required.

Instead of taking years, which undermines the process, applying for a patent was done much quicker. Now the lengthy timeframes help destroy the value of filing foreign patents.

There should also be a simpler method for describing a software patent – something like, "It will do A, B, and C, its unique features are D and E, and its advantages are F and G." Those changes would reduce the number of lawyers and simplify the language.

The SCOTUS members had no understanding of software applications, at least not to the level where they could intelligently make rulings. When they ask questions, they are blindly influenced. Justices don't understand software versus hardware technology, and neither does the public.

If you don't understand databases and communications, and you don't possess multiple software patents, you need to listen. That applies to law firms representing major energy firms, the military, religious groups, and politicians.

Even the FCC is obsolete; communications has become software-driven. I believe the solution is to have a very technical international group for deciding issues on software patents and virtual networks. I also believe the relative value of software patents should be reduced, especially in the case of very powerful patents. Software patents should not restrict the system.

Instead of discussing how to define a robust system that doesn't destroy society, the super-power leaders are content to play world-order games and reward their incompetent associates. As an expanded example, I noticed two people were playing online poker offered by a Chinese company. The website was pppoker. On the Internet, it was referred to as a "cooperation" run by AceKing Tech Limited, a multinational technology group registered in the UK.

This website used small card rooms and bookies to collect cash from online players. Pppoker "operated" in the U.S., albeit they are set up offshore.

Were the British paid off to help to disguise ownership? British places like Gibraltar or the Isle of Mann should have no authority to approve anything related to U.S. online poker. Instead, the British colonies have created a tariff to restrict U.S. creativity. This is unfair to U.S. citizens, but unless Congressmen can help the wealthy U.S. casino owners or the European oligarchs who control the foreign entertainment industry, they ignore non-elite U.S. citizens.

I write authoritatively because I believe I have written the two most important on-line poker patents in the world. I have some abstract vision in the virtual space.

When I got my first online poker patent, Jim Baker's law firm, Baker-Botts, handled the application. As soon as the GOP Senate passed the bill to halt online poker in the U.S., I had to get a new patent firm. I took this to mean the Christian Republicans were negative on the online-poker issue because of their mafias and the religious groups. Did this mean Baker-Botts had to go with the GOP initiative to allow the British to control online gambling?

Casino owners like Shelton Adelson and Tilman Fertitta care less about poker other than they want their revenue interests protected. They want a mafia monopoly!

The Queen of England must share similar interests. The English influence a number of nations, and English oligarchs believe they should be the "authority" on many international matters, including online poker.

Queen Elizabeth is part of the World-Order game. She never played good Texas Hold'em, but she's taken advantage of the U.S. non-elites like me. The Queen has no clue about technology and in a fair world she should have been taken to court. Unfortunately, the U.S. oligarchs support the English oligarchs and both groups support the international mafias.

The International Game Technology [IGT], an Italian company, owns the majority of the hardware patents for slot machines. They may have a monopoly in U.S. slot-machine patents.

IGT's hardware concepts are patentable even though more flexible software concepts are blocked. This is a biased arrangement the DOJ and SCOTUS support. IGT is a corporation supporting the mafia owned casinos. Their hardware slot-machine patents need to be re-evaluated in light of digital software. Software patents must be allowed precedence!

We laud our patent system, but because international oligarchs are only interested in maintaining their interests, the patent process no longer rewards the individual inventor.

Software patents are dangerous because they are so powerful. That bothers the elites. The elites want a patent system so they can use corporations to acquire a monopoly of patents in an area. Any patents they can't buy, they will legislate as being illegal, or they will pass restrictive legislation to control the revenues. The patent system has become too slow, too expensive, and too restrictive.

This international elite linkage occurs in all industries. Gambling revenues are probably small compared to the potential savings in the pharmaceutical and health care industries.

For decades, Republicans have had ownership in the medical industry. They participated in the profits, and they passed laws to continue to inflate costs. The elite middlemen, the lawyers and insurance companies, inflated our medical bills.

The conflicting SCOTUS agenda means a non-elite person has little chance to win in a conflict. The U.S. is biased to support the Allied elites, which include people like Queen Elizabeth. That's why adversarial nations like China and Russia ignore patents.

When this explanation of the SCOTUS illegality is extended, it means the U.S. government is based on fraud, the scheming of the incompetent elite. That's part of the reason the public can't get information out of the DOJ. Who does someone ask a question? People are expected to obey the law, but what is the law and who defined it? In many cases, some DOJ lawyers wrote an opinion that supported the President's wishes and that opinion was for the elites who gave money to the president's campaign.

In the gambling area, the mafias define the rules or laws so they can have a monopoly that allows them to stay in power. The mafias are not creative giants and software is not their tool. Without a static system, the [hardware] slot machines would be antiquated.

The intelligence communities are tied to the mafias and they are an example of planned complexity. Homeland Security was set up as a new vehicle for the CIA to have more power that wouldn't look like it fell under their umbrella. This organization allows Homeland Security to influence media and politics. The CIA wouldn't be able to do this because they are not supposed to operate domestically. That may be the main reason we have over a dozen *intelligence* agencies.

Don't think for one minute that these intelligence organizations don't all go back to one powerful set of individuals. If that wasn't the case, Clapper would have been gone a long time ago. Control is collusive and the power is in different areas. Did you see the movie *Vice*?

When you hear the CIA's motto, laugh. "Ye shall know the truth, and the truth will make you free." The CIA is the biggest liar, thief, and drug smuggler on the planet. One can never tell if they are spreading truth or fabricating a story.

The public needs truth. Both parties need to purge 90% of their Congressmen. The public needs solid technical and logical candidates who are honest, thinking managers. The candidates need to be anti-racist and not clannish.

The shift to digital will improve the functionality of society. With faster communications, there is a software-driven world on our doorstep. The U.S. could soon see the optimization of society. Politics shouldn't dictate the future. Digital technology should be used to refine our system and get rid of bankers, lawyers, and politicians.

SCOTUS needs to fix its patent deficiency by vesting the authority in a capable group and acknowledging their opinions should be fair to non-elite individuals as opposed to elites or big corporations. For instance, ARPA services the Deep State. I knew an English engineer with a Ph.D. in mechanical engineering who patented in the U.S. a robot that could propel itself through water, drive over land, and fly over obstacles. This robot was ideally suited for the military.

Another firm began filed patents with seemingly older technology and they received government contracts. The engineer called the president of the other firm using a false name and asked about their patents. The president had military contacts and his firm had received a $500,000 grant from ARPA to secure patents in 50 countries. He was part of the good-old-boy system.

Rule 21: Instead of an elite hierarchy controlling the public, a new future should be designed by honest scholars, technicians, and intellectuals. The Government needs to be completely restructured. Congress needs fixing. Too many non-technical lawyers - no problem solvers!

Facebook has a problem. I am sure there is a work-around, but others can propose better solutions.

It's time to fire the Pope and the Queen and let everyone know who has the money/assets and where they are.

Climate Change and Covid-19

History teaches that in the distant past, many smaller groups of people and nations disappeared when the climate changed and became more adverse. It happens periodically, and change is seldom a complete surprise. The most obvious change will be the weather and the oceans.

When I hunted deer in the 1950s, it rained regularly. We would plant oats a few weeks before the hunting season and expect to get rain. Right before the season opened, a big cold front would arrive as if scheduled. The heavy rains and cooler weather would be perfect. The flounder would leave the bays and run along on the coast.

Now our weather has changed. The rain may or may not show up. Sometimes there doesn't seem to be a flounder run. It doesn't get as cold. Our winters can be mild.

Around 1990, I remember sitting in a tree stand near New Ulm, Texas. It was the driest and mildest winter I had ever seen. I thought, "These post oak woods will be replaced with mesquite trees." That hasn't yet happened where I was hunting, but it is happening in many places around Fayette County.

In the summer of 2012, I took an Advanced Course offered by the Landmark organization. The instructor had just returned from a two week trip to the Arctic. He had been with a dozen PhD's studying climate change. The team of scientists was astonished by the speed of the ice melt. They changed prior predictions that the ice would melt by 2030 to the ice melting by 2025.

In July 2015, James Hansen and 16 other climate experts released a research paper that said the seas could rise 10 feet in 50 to 85 years – much more than the 2.6 feet that had been projected for 2100. If their report is correct, a lot of coastal residences will be destroyed.

California has been having dry spells since 2016 and the northern Pacific Ocean has been warming.

2019 brought disastrous fires to Australia, and the United States had the weirdest weather I've ever seen. In Texas, it was extremely mild in November, December, January, and February. We had no winter. I watched the weather radar and there was almost no moisture between northern California and Florida for weeks at a time. It was like it was programmed. That worked out great because the Coronavirus got here late and for a while, it was almost a non-event.

Then, there was a rash of fires along the West Coast. Washington, Oregon, and California were hit with hundreds of fires. Those fires were easy to set because the woods were dry. The snowfall had disappeared.

What is even more alarming is the September 2020 report that the Thwaites, a Britain-sized glacier in Antarctica, is melting at an alarming rate and the scientists cannot exactly model how the glacier will break up and melt because the undersea currents are unpredictable. If everything melts, hundreds of years from now the seas will have risen 200 feet.

Climate scientists have yet to prove they have global warming correctly calculated. The average temperature could more quickly warm and the sea levels could rise quicker than forecast. It's not an exact science. A lot of property would be for sale in Miami, New York, New Orleans, Corpus Christi, and Rockport.

I am not going out on a limb and predict, but that's a possible trend and the public tends to ignore the worst possible case. The climate experts have been off in their projections in the past and the fires in Australia and the West Coast may have been an early warning.

Because of the way the fires occurred, I think the West Coast fires were man-made in most cases. I also think only one group would have the power and lack of conscience to set those fires.

Exxon has been an outstanding corporation, but their interest is not in the national interest. For decades, oil companies have worked to dampen the global warming message. They got their wish when President George W. Bush supported anything the energy elites had to say.

I skim on this subject because what George W. Bush and Donald Trump did was almost criminal. This is not a win-win subject for a conservative, but it would not be a question for a Teddy Roosevelt.

One problem today is that we have presidents that have never really been close to nature and we have so much concentrated wealth. I don't like Bill Gates owning 260,000 acres of farmland and wanting to make money from the Covid-19 virus. I don't trust him.

Covid-19 seemed programmed. It appeared at the right time and it should have been a non-event. At first, it affected the younger than 50 Chinese who were two heavy smokers. That portion of society was hard hit because their lungs are susceptible to pneumonia.

Early on, China and Italy had the biggest number of cases. There were supposed to be a lot of Chinese who vacationed in Italy. There was a rumor that both had massive problems because of their heavy pollution, which was not good for the lungs.

There was also a rumor that several nations listed the cause of other deaths like cancer to have been Coronavirus. The U.S. hospitals could make more federal money from a Coronavirus death.

Until June 2020, the U.S. had lost 100,000 people out of 320M. That's less than .04%.

When the Covid-19 appeared, hell broke loose. The economy came to a halt. People were afraid to drive on the freeways. The Saudis and the Russians failed to close their pipeline valves and crude fell to below $20 a barrel because the airlines lost most of their passengers.

The stock market went into free-fall. Senator Diane Feinstein and three other senators were found to be trading stock on inside intelligence reports. This sort of thing has been going on ever since the Reagan administration in the 1980s. Bob Woodward wrote a book titled *Veil* discussing how CIA Director William Casey tuned into intelligence reports to find investments.

Feinstein and three other senators traded hundreds of thousands of shares long and short and that equated to millions of dollars. The four senators may have been the tip of the iceberg of people trading off of intelligence data.

This was high drama! Will the economy collapse? Are elites pulling the scheme of schemes?

Everything is about control of something. It helps to be able to predict and control the weather. I noticed forecasters are fairly accurately predicting the weather four days in advance. The intelligence services must have great models of patterns and tremendous computer power as well as a large number of tracking stations.

The government's ability to accurately forecast weather showed up when they forecast Hurricane Harvey to landfall at Rockport, Texas, proceed inland toward Austin, backtrack to Rockport, and then head for Houston. This weather pattern took several days and there was record rainfall – past 50 inches in some places.

The public has forgotten this incredibly unique pattern was forecast days in advance. It was a black swan weather event that never could have been forecast before.

If a group can forecast weather patterns, wouldn't it be something if they could create weather patterns? I found the weather patterns in the winter of 2019-2020 to be strangely quite different from the normal. We had the warmest winter in our recorded history.

Starting in November, I closely watched Accuweather and noticed there was no appreciable rainfall between California and Florida. This pattern persisted through March.

When strange events occur, there is a way to make money if you know in advance. In this case, the price of natural gas in dead winter fell to $1.75 an MCF. The price of natural gas would normally go up to above $3 an MCF. The bullish speculators were slaughtered by this weather pattern. Buy low and sell high failed. Was the weather re-programmed?

What if a country could control the weather and develop and release a custom virus that took out old people and smokers? Wouldn't that be an interesting weapon? "Hey, bow down or the next round will really be fatal!"

Years ago, when I released my first JFK book, I had a small display at the JFK convention in Dallas. I was alone a gentleman came up and he told me about his friend, a CIA agent. His friend told him on his deathbed that AIDs was a CIA experiment that escaped to the monkeys in Africa.

I did extensive research and that conversation rang true, but it got suppressed; a great book on the subject just disappeared.

By my nature, I connect dots and speculate on "What-ifs" of the U.S. military doing medical experiments. They have a history of doing this type of research.

I was surprised to read that a large percentage of the flu cases had disappeared in several areas. What could have made that happen? Is there any relationship to covid-19?

It took Moderna just two days to come up with a vaccine. That was in January 2020, and then it took 11 months to get approval. Perhaps 100,000 U.S. lives could have been saved.

Hmmm. Have I been reading too many conspiracy stories?

Rule 22: The public needs the truth about the weather, technology, science, and the future. Information is valuable and it affects investments. Information should be more open source. Why should a few corporations controlled by the

oligarchs own everything and put the people out of work when
the computers take over? It doesn't make sense.

Don't get too involved in conspiracy theories.

Square Johns and Assassins

A square John is an underworld term for a sheep. If you take slot machines, a square John will be pulling the arm of a quarter slot-machine. He is a regular worker and likes to relax on weekends.

As opposed to a square John, a whale doesn't have to work. He might be in a fine, enclosed room pulling the arm of a $500 slot.

If we were looking at sports betting, the square John might be losing maybe $10,000 a year. For that, on weekends he watches game after game for three-hour intervals where he perhaps wagers $100 a game. He loves the excitement of the game and the rush of the wagers. His wife might even make bets if she has a good job.

What happened to poker is interesting. It used to be poker and sports betting were kind of grouped together. Poker in the card room was dealt at a rate of about 25 hands an hour. A dealer had to shuffle the cards and cut them.

In the 2000-2014 timeframe, online poker came into being. When online poker was released it played at 60 to 100 hands an hour. With improved systems, 150 to 200 hands an hour became possible.

At the 25 hands an hour level, there would be 9 players at a table and a player might get one monster hand an hour. If the player played 200 hands an hour online, he might get 7 or 8 good hands an hour.

A poker hand normally has four rounds - the pre-flop, the flop, the turn, and the river. Creative software people perfected robots that would play the pre-flop perfectly. Once a decent drawing hand showed up, a professional player could finish the action after the flop. If a professional put up eighteen robots playing at the same time, then he could play maybe 3,000 hands an hour and play 100 quality hands an hour. The player went from the back roads to the freeway.

Some online operations recognized this early on and put their professionals to using robots. They separated poker from the other action and helped destroy poker because sports-betting was more lucrative and poker was self-defeating.

They found they couldn't control the U.S. poker professional, so they outlawed online poker in the U.S. "If we don't profit from online poker, you non-elites don't profit from it either."

The combination of a robot and a professional produced a much better player and soon the square Johns were losing consistently and not feeling the love. Because they are a somewhat addictive group, many poker players moved to sports betting. In the process, the casinos got rid of competition, the professional online poker players and their robots.

If you have noticed, bars with drinks and girls, like Hooters and Twin Peaks, have gone to beautiful women who wear shorts and sell food and drinks in an environment with unlimited large-screen TVs that pick up all the sporting events. This is similar to the sports betting paradigm. Grab the square John for three hours of sports on TV and sell him drinks and food. The girls are a side attraction.

That's what the media and political game have gone to. Grab someone's attention for two or three hours so you can influence his vote and get him to pass a story to his peer group. Make the announcers beautiful women, different ethnic groups, celebrities, and others. Have them articulate some outrageous story, some fake news the audience can share with other sheep. This is what everything has gone to.

When you get the square Johns in your tent, you start to also bring in a few whales. That's where the big money is, the person who can bet the $500,000 on the Super bowl and afford to lose it.

Little Larry Culbreath was a famous assassin from the 1960s. He ran with the Overton gang and killed federal judge *Maximum* John Wood Jr. Charles Harrelson took the wrap for the Wood murder.

Little Larry also murdered Tim Overton and his girlfriend, for which he received no jail time. All of this was written up in multiple books. *JFK and the World Oligarchy* had a chapter titled *Little Larry Culbreath*.

In 2020, I was sitting in a Texas Hold'em game in a Houston card room. Jay Pollard came over and motioned me aside to ask, "Do you know 'Little' Larry sitting across from you?"

Jay had once played in a card game with Sammy Patrenella. Sammy owned the popular Italian restaurant Patrenella's, and Sammy introduced Jay to Little Larry. On the side, Sammy told Jay, "You need to avoid Little Larry. He's a stone-cold killer."

Sammy's family restaurant had great Italian food and pictures of the Lyndon and Ladybird Johnson, the Bushes, and famous poker players of the era that came out of Houston, like Tree Top Strauss and Johnny Bonetti. I had met Strauss and my deceased friend Raymon Poland knew Strauss well.

Sammy's wife Josephine used to love to play in Jay's game. She was a tremendous lady. If we went to Patrenella's for food, Josephine always brought us a dish of olives to go with that to-die-for bread.

Sammy Patrenella is pictured in one of the earliest World Series of Poker group photos. Patrenella is listed as "Sammy ?". He is standing next to David Baxter, another Texas player. A story Sammy once told was that he and Tree Top were leaving the Nugget in Vegas and as they walked out a person came up to Strauss and said, "Tree Top, my cards have been running cold. Can you loan me a couple of dollars?"

Strauss peeled off a hundred-dollar bill and handed it to the man. As they walked away, Sammy inquired about whether the borrower was a friend of Strauss. Tree Top replied, "If I knew him, I would have given him $200."

I should have recognized Little Larry, but it had been 60 years. The last time I saw Larry, he was proud of his sawed-off shotgun.

Fortunately, he didn't recognize me either, but I should have realized the player was Little Larry by how he acted. He got into a verbal debate with the dealer and threatened him. He talked for a long time with another player running a card room in Victoria, Texas. In his conversation, he mentioned playing with the deceased Bobby Hoff.

Bobby Hoff was a semi-famous poker player from Victoria. He went to the University of Texas for a brief time before going to Vegas. I had met Bobby Hoff, David Baxter, Tim Overton, and Little Larry all about the same time.

In another poker session, I took a picture of this Little Larry and tried to ID him. He was going under a different name and my one other source could not identify him from the picture. That didn't matter. As luck would have it, one day Little Larry was seated next to me on my right.

My turn-on for the night was when Larry looked at me and said, "Lawyer So-and-so thinks So-and-so is an FBI snitch."

In my oligarchy book, I discuss being told that Larry was a snitch. It was natural for me to look Larry in the eye and respond, "I heard Little Larry was a snitch."

Larry replied, "I can't speak for Little Larry."

I wish I had added, "Well, I thought you knew everybody."

I asked Little Larry about a lot of the old Austin players, and he spoke freely about anyone you might mention. I avoided asking about a few people because they would have been too close to home.

On the subject of Sammy Patrenella, he said Sammy's daughter had gone to an East Coast college [like Harvard] and she had met and married a Jewish boy from one of the richest families in Europe. It sounded like Schnitzer. I guess Sammy taught his daughter the concept of marriage-mergers.

Little Larry walking out in the open with a new identity means he is protected. It wouldn't be a situation I would inquire about. Fortunately, since then that card-room has halted their card games.

The military-mafia relationship is also always in place. This agreement to work together has allowed the Jewish, Italian, and Anglo mafia chiefs to dominate gambling and entertainment in Allied countries. These groups work together because smuggling drugs and guns, laundering money, and avoiding taxes have always been prized talents of the elites.

The U.S. government is influenced by the mafias. President Trump had casino connections. Casino connections are Mafia connections because an Italian company, IGT, owns the majority of the hardware patents for slot-machines.

IGT makes it possible for the Italian Mafia to control the U.S. casino market. Success in the casino business is based on a casinos' ability to get authorization to have more slot-machines than their competition.

President Trump invited Tilman Fertitta to the White House to discuss turning the economy around. Fertitta owns casinos and has fancy steak houses in Trump's developments.

A subsequent chapter in this book discusses why Tilman may run for President as a Democrat in 2024, if Tilman's businesses recover from the pandemic. Tilman did everything he could to help Trump win. Trump would reciprocate in 2024 – tit for tat if it would help and make some money. That probably won't happen because in politics, once a loser, always a loser.

Why would Tilman Fertitta consider running for President? A brain-dead Joe Biden facilitates everybody's run for President. This scenario provides a lot of options.

In Texas, in the last five years, "legal" card-rooms have sprung up. The Houston area has seen perhaps ten different card-rooms. The top card rooms are near mid-town and a few miles from each other. They offered drinks, food, and a reasonably plush environment. They appear to have Las Vegas connections and they are in fierce competition. Do they represent the various mafias?

They are here because they understand the business and have big money behind them. Houston is as Hunter S. Thompson described — an edgy oil town on a bayou where everything is for sale.

Rule 24: For obvious reasons, don't be a Square John.

2020 started with a bang when Iranian General Qasem Solemaini was taken out by a U.S. drone at the Bagdad Airport. President Trump's media explained the assassination was an ending for an Iranian who liked to kill Americans.

It seemed strange how Iraq embraced Solemaini. Iraq and Iran had fought a bitter war just three decades earlier, but Iraq asked the U.S. military to leave. The Middle East people weren't feeling the love from the U.S. Perhaps they thought we had overstayed or all we wanted was their oil and control.

Washington responded, "We're not about to leave. We need to control the oil and install our NWO."

There was also a rumor some elites made millions from the general's assassination when the price of crude surged and turned the shorts around.

If you are from the world's center of exploration, Houston, you may understand the oil and gas markets. It is easy to make money trading crude and natural gas. Buy low and sell high, and have the right connections. That always works.

Oil is a commodity the U.S has controlled since WW II because we use so much energy. We're energy pigs; we can't live without controlling the markets. That means a few Allied elites have to control the refineries and the technology to build them.

Was Solemaini's assassination for money? I got kind of a confirmation, but you know rumors abound. Some are fake news. Too many people are tied to the Deep State, and sometimes they shade the truth.

Six months earlier there had been a different rumor - that war with Iran was coming, but after the assassination of Solemaini it was apparent Trump didn't want to escalate, at least not in early 2020. Perhaps the military was saving the ammunition for after the presidential election.

During January 2020, Trump's impeachment proceedings were a struggle for control. The GOP senators backed Trump to remain leaders of their state's party, and the lawyers lined up at the feeding trough.

Right or wrong, the elites always win! Look at the way the lawyers flip-flopped between the Bill Clinton and Donald Trump impeachments. Lindsey Graham and Alan Dershowitz were perfect examples. "Yes, I said that, but this is a different situation. There are compelling circumstances and arguments to believe the opposite."

Ron Paul never got much done in Congress, but since Paul left Congress and he took an active role as a libertarian and appeared as a friend of Lew Rockwell. In January 2020, in an interview, Ron Paul discussed how the CIA had to be the major JFK assassin. Paul was very articulate. I don't recall Paul discussing this subject while he was in Congress. He is probably trying to help his son Rand gain traction.

After Donald Trump was acquitted by the Senate, Rand Paul named Trump's whistleblower. A person outing whistleblowers is usually trying to bias the public. Rand Paul was trying to line up Trump's support so he could run for president in 2024.

Whistleblowers try to make our crooked system honest. As noted previously, local police are not in a position to help the public, and newspaper editorials are now worthless. Our social structures are hierarchical, and no one is policing the system for the public's benefit.

In the 2020 presidential election, the Democrats seemed short-handed. They had many candidates, but they lacked a younger, charismatic leader like a Cuban or a Cuomo or a Kennedy.

Mr. gun-control Michael Bloomberg thought he sensed an opportunity to buy his way in. Instead, he couldn't buy the

Democratic nomination and he made a fool of himself. A lot of people want to keep their guns.

Longevity and prior experience normally count in Democratic politics. Bernie paid his dues in the 2016 campaign and he started strong. He was hoping the super-delegates couldn't organize and push him aside this time.

My prime forecaster and world-class JFK SME, Robert P. Morrow, said there would be an exceptional turnout, around 70%, and because people are so turned off it would be in Biden's favor. He said I could get good odds since the impeachment trial was over.

One of my great doctors knew Biden's doctor and he was told Biden lost his memory due to the same kind of stroke that killed his son. Who would allow a mentally impaired person to run? Who could push brain-dead Biden to the top? The answer is the oligarchs. Biden will be easy to manipulate, and he also supports Israel and the Catholics.

Donald Trump must have thought Joe Biden would be the easiest opponent, so he was behind Biden.

After she lost, the candidates hated Hillary because she was a loser.

I didn't understand why a lot of seniors supported Trump. He implied he would decrease social security benefits if he got another term. And, why would the public want Kushner to be throwing more money at consulting firms like McKinsey & Company? Did he get free consulting from those firms?

Is there any group whose support Trump and Kushner didn't try to influence? Every time you viewed the Internet, Trump wanted approval and he was an expert on everything.

Before the election, Ann Coulter let her fangs out and went against Trump for outing Jeff Sessions; Mattis tried to act authoritatively; then Bolton took his knife out. "Et too Bolton?" Finally, Kellyanne Conway left the ship.

The 2020 election turned out precisely as rumored, but I could not predict. I had to ask SMEs I knew. All I can predict is that politics are like a football game. Tune in when there are three minutes left of the fourth quarter.

It was rumored Mr. Tilman Fertitta owned some property between Cat Springs and New Ulm, and that he once stopped in Fayetteville at Orsak's. Supposedly, Tilman told Ike Orsak how restaurants should cook steaks. Perhaps Tilman didn't appreciate the great chicken-fried steaks with Orsak's thick cream gravy.

Tilman Fertitta is a master in the restaurant and casino industries. Mr. Fertitta owns the Golden Nugget Casinos and Landry's Seafood. His forte is putting together successful restaurant and casino deals.

Tilman never made a bad deal. At the same time, investors were sometimes left sucking air. Tilman amassed a fortune in his deals, but very few others made money in a Tilman Fertitta deal. From what I have heard, that included Floyd Landry and Buster Hennessey.

In 2019, Tilman Fertitta released a biography titled *Shut Up and Listen*. The title of Tilman's book defines how Tilman runs his organization. The title could have been titled, "*Bow, and do what I tell you.*"

Tilman's book made it sound like he was the person being squeezed, but it's always the other way around. Tilman is notorious for squeezing every dime he can out of vendors and investors.

Tilman was worth billions and he associated with scores of powerful people. For instance, Tilman was close to the Clintons and Gabrielle [Gabby] Giffords. When Bill Clinton ran for president, the Fertittas sponsored a $10,000 a plate dinner for the Clintons and the Clintons stayed at Fertitta's home.

When voters endorsed casino owner Donald Trump as President, they invited the casino owners and their lawyers to run the country. The casino owners are mafia, and to think otherwise is ridiculous.

Tilman Fertitta professes to be a capitalist and not be a socialist. On television his bold political statement seemed to be, "Here comes Fertitta, a conservative Democrat."

Everyone from Houston knows Tilman's ego is a thousand miles wide and running for President was a reason for him to release a biography. Tilman's book garnered name recognition and it was worth a read just to get a view of the man.

Tilman's book was a regurgitation of business basics. It emphasized knowing a business's numbers and offering customer hospitality, which can be referred to as customer service. Those elements are the most important aspects of operating a successful business. If you don't know the numbers, you can't run a successful business, and if you don't offer good customer service, you will lose business.

Years ago, I was in Tilman's Golden Nugget in Lake Charles. I was very thirsty and wanted some water. Almost all the casinos have a water fountain somewhere. I asked around, but I couldn't find one in the Nugget. I wound up going into an expensive club and asking to buy some water. The club didn't sell water, but the manager got me a large glass of cool water, at no charge. In the following years, when I was asked about the Lake Charles Nugget, I always said, "They have great customer service and they charge for everything, except water."

Shut Up and Listen also has a wonderful chapter describing the hard times that Tilman went through in Houston between 1980 and 1989 when 25% of the Texas banks' assets dried up. Nine out of the ten biggest commercial banks failed. Every savings and loan failed. Every new housing development had a litter of unoccupied houses.

Texas went from where 1,000 people a week were moving into the state to where people were fleeing, leaving foreclosures behind. Businesses collapsed and new housing developments failed.

The price of oil created the boom because Houston was the oil exploration capital of the world. When the tax incentive for drilling wells was taken away, it took the banks down with the smaller oil companies. When the U.S. government passed legislation that took away some of the oil company write-offs, the major oil companies cut their U.S. exploration programs at the end of the year, around 1982.

Tilman's book gives away few secrets of how Tilman views the details of his restaurant success beyond the general big pictures. For instance, in 2014, Tilman's restaurants generally handled seafood and steaks. To my knowledge, Tilman's restaurants never do BBQ. I assume that's because BBQ is too competitive in Texas and it must not be what Tilman is looking for, which might be a higher price for steaks in a more opulent setting or the ability to have more control of revenues by connecting to the shrimp fleets.

Tilman didn't discuss the details of his restaurant theories with the general public because he never gives anything away. For that very reason, Tilman has the potential to be a great leader in the mode of a controlled Donald Trump. Tilman is a constrained decision-maker who never tweets at 3 AM and rarely makes a mistake.

Before Covid-19 hit, Tilman acquired the Houston Rockets basketball team by taking out a $2B loan. Tilman also owned the Nugget casinos in several states, beginning with Louisiana. He owned the Nugget in Las Vegas, Nevada, and his close relatives, also named Fertitta, owned several casinos in Nevada. If you go to Biloxi or Atlantic City, Tilman Fertitta was again represented.

Donald Trump's success surely helped embolden Tilman Fertitta. Tilman was more successful than Trump; Tilman could see he *had* a little more money than Donald Trump, and he loved to make decisions. Tilman is a proven winner and Donald Trump opened the door as a casino owner who won the presidency.

Because Tilman controlled 600 quality steak and seafood restaurants and casinos, he was in an ideal position to offer upper-crust clients an integrated environment for eating and placing sports bets.

Before the pandemic, I thought Tilman Fertitta would run for President as a Democrat in 2024. Unfortunately, because of Covid-19, Tilman's assets have suffered. His Rockets, the Golden Nugget casinos, and his seafood and steak houses had to shut down for a while. Tilman went to the financial markets to raise a trillion dollars. Now Tilman and Trump may be cornered.

Regardless of who becomes President, the elites must ensure they control his action. A new president will make sure the FED and the Deep State can continue to safeguard the elites' assets. The right Democrat or Republican is the elites' answer.

The oligarchs have to control the presidency, and the president must love Israel. Another Bush might work. Mitch McConnell might have to help get rid of Ted Cruz to make that happen. It's hard to tell what one good pandemic coupled with an attempted coup can do for the elections.

Rule 25: Don't elect presidents who associate with casino owners. They are influenced by the mafias.

Of course, in the United States the Jewish and Catholic clans are connected to the mafias, and the candidates generally support Israel and Christian religions. So, you don't get much of a choice.

The Future

Today, one needs to consider where they are and plan accordingly.

There is a southerly migration of the population; the high tax structures and climate will take a toll on some cities and states. People and businesses are exiting California because of high taxes and restrictions. People are leaving New York, Chicago, and Detroit.

The Republican and Democratic parties waited until the last minute to solve the problems caused by Coronavirus. Both parties struggled for position so they could make the other party out to be inadequate. Trump missed on Covid-19, and Biden assured the Democratic sheep it couldn't have been done without them.

The CIA sees daylight breaking. There is no way they can backtrack. They have only one choice - they must push Iran aside. The Muslims are too religious, don't have enough weapons, and they regard women as non-beings. They will try to maintain control, but historically they always lose. They will be forced to shut up and sit down.

The U.S. is set for inflation. The next generation will be controlled by our national debt and the inflation cooked into the books. The lower-class will be tied down forever. This is classic communism. Karl Marx and Friedrich Engels would be proud.

The elites love inflation. The rich own a piece of the pie, and they always receive a disproportionate return from inflation. This inflation problem is not a Republican or a Democrat problem. There is no "political party," but there is a "club". The clubs' elite members don't think. They assume they're brilliant. They can be right-wing or left-wing. They lie and coordinate with the other club elites.

If you talk with a well-off GOP person and you say, "Hey, we need to balance the budget," he'll reply: "No! The

U.S. has gone past that. We can't possibly balance the budget."

That same person will complain of the aliens and the welfare crowd, but he wants more people because he has to have inflation. He has a big house. He has to have that $250K tax write-off when he sells his house. It's part of the game.

Granted, inflation has somewhat been held down because real wages have not kept up, but a smart person will get as good an education as he can afford, buy as large a house as he can in a growing neighborhood, and then after seven or eight years sell in the spring and buy a bigger house to take advantage of the tax program.

All these big low-rent apartment units for older citizens that are guaranteed by the government are a typical example. Those apartments are everywhere, even in the backwaters of Montana. The government authorized those so the rich could get another tax break.

A person has to be financially conservative. He or she should maintain patience and look for good deals. Try to understand basics like construction and real estate.

Most importantly, do things you love and find the right spouse. Marriage has to be a team. You need to program your lifestyle so you and your family can enjoy life.

People need to find their passion, assuming it allows them a reasonable living. Work with your significant other and do the activities that satisfy your expectations. Love doing activities that are good for both of you.

A few years back I played golf with my friend Tommy Ellis. I asked him, "Tommy, you are always playing poker and golf. Why do you do it?"

His answer was simple, "I love it."

There is no rocket science here. Successful people run, ski, or hike several miles a day. They do their activity where they want to do it. They made their money, and they can afford to do things they love. Some really intelligent people walk the golf courses pushing their golf cart five days a week. They believe staying in shape will allow them to live longer and it makes them feel great. They love the emotional high it gives them.

Your job should be something you can do well. People enjoy their job more if they are good at it. It's easier to work longer and concentrate more when you like something.

If you don't like your job, one choice is to try to reinvent the job such that it is more enjoyable. I met a person who was a great mechanical engineer and developer. He went to work for Schwinn, a major bicycle manufacturer. One day his boss, the chief design engineer, asked him to fill out a description of what he would like to do. Afterward, his boss came back to him and commented. "I see you want my job."

When I met this person, he ran his own custom bicycle manufacturing company. I assume he accomplished his passion.

Make health a priority. As one ages, mobility will be critical. Lose your mobility and you are as well as dead. There's no reason not to learn the basics of keeping your body in reasonable shape. Before you get too old, get into several types of simple exercises that let you stretch and tone your muscles. Learn to walk, or do yoga, or even just some simple isometrics. You will feel so much better and it's a big part of enjoying life.

When I was in my late thirties, I picked up a heavy ice chest and it hurt my back. Then, occasionally my back would seem to jerk out of position. Once I drove a golf ball and threw my back out on the very first hole.

I went to see a back specialist. She showed me all the x-rays and convinced me that I had no serious problems. My problem was that I didn't do proper back exercises to keep my core muscles in shape.

Every few days, I did a brief set of isometric exercises to strengthen my back muscles. My exercises were simple. When I woke up in the morning, as I lay there in bed, I tensed my legs in all kinds of directions. I would move my big feet to make a "V" and then put them together and go from side to side as I lie there. Within two months, my back problems were gone. I haven't had any problems since. I moved next to a golf course. Whenever the weather accommodated, I played.

My story isn't unique. I saw an associate named Ron who loves to ski. Ron does a similar set of back exercises every morning. When he wakes up, while he is lying in bed, he begins leg exercises, moving one leg over the other. Ron learned to exercise his core back muscles early in life and now he lives in Tahoe and skis 4-5 hours a day.

Even when you are just sitting in a chair, if you raise one leg and hold it for a short time, that's good exercise. And when you walk, if you raise your leg higher each time you step forward, that's exercise. Exercise can be simple and for a short period. I like squats to firm up the legs and back.

Make your "bucket" list. Find something you love that is good for you. Buy a house next to the ski slope, golf course, or a lake or a trout stream. Encourage your spouse to join you in planning your great adventure. There are plenty of locations where you can both do what you love.

Get in an industry you can work in even when you're 80. You won't be doing delivery for Amazon at 70. You are only going to live so long, and at some point, you strangely and quickly turn *old*, like a tree blossoming.

When my father approached 90, I asked him, "How long is it good?" He replied, "Until you are about 75."

I asked the same question to one of my Aunt Josie before she became senile. She gave me the same response.

One of my friends passed 80. For years he was the manager of a large group of writers. He regularly gave conferences, and he published four books. He was still strong and loved what he did, but he decided his cutoff was 80. Now he focuses more on a little writing and the management of his group has passed on to a younger writer.

The age range of 70 to 85 is a range where it becomes more difficult to function. You won't understand until it happens, but you owe it to yourself to do the things you love, especially if that forces you to stay in better shape.

Gold and silver? When an investment advisor tells a reader to diversify by buying 10 to 20% of his money in gold or silver, I set his book aside. Who knows? People may mine gold off some planet or change the rules of the game. Do you believe there is any gold left in Fort Knox?

Stay diversified and have some liquid funds. Buy low on weakness and sell high; have a few good connections to run your thoughts by.

I believe an average investor can't profitably *trade* equities, futures, and 3X ETFs. The markets are too competitive; there are too many professionals using computers, and the markets are manipulated.

Professional trading groups use dynamic algorithms that qualify the systems as AI systems. Most of the time their winnings are marginal because the markets are competitive, but after a dozen or so years, some of the great technical people come up with systems that consistently work well.

The Medallion fund is an example of a successful trading fund. They have averaged around 66% profit for decades. They are a group of great mathematicians with software that looks for patterns and then trades leveraged short-term trades. They are so successful they are now closed to the public. They trade a limited amount, like $10B a year. As a trader or an investor, that's the type of competition you are competing against. That structure makes you the square John. It's self-defeating.

I worked on trading systems and I know groups that trade leveraged investments using AI type systems. Most systems hope to make 25 percent a year. Those systems are programmed to avoid that one big collapse in the market because if a trader can't, it will take years to recover the losses.

There is a battle going on. The middle-class has been destroyed by the elites and now the elites are squeezing the remaining masses for all their money. In the stock market, on one side the broker firms offer platforms to extract their pound of flesh while the traders use sophisticated trading systems that grind it out. A square John has no chance, but the market is the only game in town.

There is only so much money floating around. The easy money is gone. If the elites can't make the money in an area by unfair advantage, they will block non-elites from making money. Unless you wish to sell your deal to the elites at a discounted price, you have to avoid the trading markets, unless you are young and very bright and wish to join them.

On a broader scale, Nelson Mandela taught us that racism and imperialism were fostered by the mentality of the elite. Mandela resisted the elite sphere of influence when he discovered the right attitude and focus while he was in prison. Mandela tried and tried again, and his level of thinking stood above any thought of personal wealth.

Our dreams can be within our reach without being religious, cultist, or elitist - if we can move to the next philosophical plateau. As Gandhi said, "We must be the change we wish to see in the world."

Henry Ford went further to defined success when he said, "Most people think of it in terms of getting; success, however, begins in terms of giving."

I think Ford meant that a person has to make decisions and give his time, his sweat equity to establish himself with the ultimate dream of helping others to rise above the chaos of ordinary man.

Consider the truth in these statements by Henry Ford:

Life is a series of experiences, each one of which makes us bigger, even though sometimes it is hard to realize; everyone who keeps learning stays young; you can do anything if you have enthusiasm; failure is only the opportunity to begin again.

If you look into the future and have a great set of rules, life can be a continuous adventure.

On top feels better, but you learn more when luck goes against you. It matters how old you are and who relies on you to bring in a little extra money so they can live an easier life. When you are 80, it's hard to live off social security and support kids with personality disorders who feel embolden.

When you are on top, you have to pay the government around 25% on earnings. Then you throw your kids some money. Your golf game is good. You are liked when you pick up the tab.

When you reach retirement age, things start getting tighter. You ignore budgets and all your investments go south, and some people start disliking you. "How could you run through all that money and not have some left for me?"

Well, let's see - golf, travel, women, kids, fine food, investments, taxes, etc. Easy come, easy go!

What makes success difficult is getting old. Young people don't want to associate with old guys. It's a lot harder to do that next deal, but some people always have a lucky star. They excel for some unknown reason. They can mess up and some strange hand will lift them out of the water.

If that doesn't happen, they will find themselves in a situation where their deals and associates die off, one by one. They seem to hear people whisper, "That sorry-no-good is getting what he deserves. Couldn't happen to a nicer guy!"

The people who really have knowledge are shaken but they keep getting epiphany after epiphany. They always have one more deal they can do. Someone with money sees the same thing and they throw them an offer. All of a sudden, they keep enough of the money to live comfortably for the rest of their life.

The art of dying when you have money is the art of the deal. It is always a much better choice to die when you were held in esteem. At least a few will show at your memorial.

Now, with the pandemic pressing the economy down, you might be able to do some damage with a million dollars. People might smile when they see you. You'd have to put out a sign for the sycophants: "Will being rewritten!"

When you survive with knowledge and mobility, it's easier to laugh about it. "The rumors of my death were overrated."

Don't you love the poem "*If?*" It strikes at the heart of the issue. That why Teddy Roosevelt has always been a favorite. If a person has the capabilities, he should live life fully. What an opportunity.

Would the oligarchs have brought in Trump or Biden if they weren't going to bankrupt the U.S. dollar?

There is all this subtle complexity. What makes life doubly difficult is trying to do things which take into consideration the feelings of others.

Men are much the worst at this because their minds have inherited all those survival instincts. One has to work hard to find the common ground.

Rule 26: Build a network of family and friends. Seek advice! Exercise and do what you love!

An Evolving Long-term Solution

We've seen this game many times. It grinds tighter and tighter until something snaps or the players walk away or die. We're close to the tipping point.

Why did we allow the Catholics and the Israelis to take over the U.S.?

It was greed and lust for power. In their place, you would do the same.

With new technology, America's problems are fixable. The new electronic lie-detector machines are nearly 100% accurate if questions are clearly phrased by an experienced operator. The person taking the tests must understand the questions and the person administering the tests must be honest and experienced. The person taking the test would also have to be tested for drugs. Drugs like Quaaludes make a person happy. This allows the person to arbitrarily answer questions and pass a lie-detector test.

The public could require the elite and their Deep State to take a properly administered lie-detector test. Lest we forget: The elites, directly or indirectly, make their profits from drug and arms trade, money laundering, avoiding taxes, wars, and other nefarious schemes. They are a group of thieves whose purpose is to run the world.

If our scholars did the right re-calibration, they could clean up the whole system. Let me guess. No one has mentioned this possibility to you. The Deep State hasn't shouted, "Hey, we have an opportunity to clean up the system!"

The leaders of the sheep need to push the passive sheep aside. The crippled sheep are not going to challenge society because they've been defeated. They try to maintain their ego. They allude to the fact that they know very little. They don't have the big picture.

Think about the marvelous potential future the world has if the public works together. Thinkers can accomplish great things.

The elites are like deer going down the same trail day after day. They are greedy and steal everything they can and they dare the public to stop them. The sheep simply need to understand the game. Digital technology is the elite's Achilles' heel, but the sheep have to see the game and want to improve their lot.

Richard Falk's *Power Shift on the New Global Order* grasps our dilemma: "... I have little doubt that those 'realists' we rely upon as dutiful, taxpaying citizens are leading us down a path heading toward doomsday. It is time we shifted our alliances and energies to the citizen pilgrims among us who are pointing us toward a humane and sustainable future for life on planet earth."

Falk goes on, "... the challenge is not just a matter of supporting humane and sensible policies, it is also a question of *structure* that allows problems to be addressed from global and human perspectives, thereby superseding national, religious, civilizational, and ethnic perspectives." [Y49]

The sheep could begin to rework this dysfunctional society and establish an enjoyable world, but the sheep are convinced they need the elites. As Hunter S. Thompson may have discovered, truth doesn't buy much at the sheeple level.

If the public hears the correct tune, they may visualize the social structure the elites have put into place. Digital systems control our lives and the elites use software to strip-mine society. In the future, a network of integrated systems could run the planet without politicians, military leaders, stockbrokers, religious leaders, lawyers, etc.

Read and extend your perspective. That will enhance your self-assurance. Remain conservative and make as much money as you can. Don't give the politicians any credit. Do your evaluation of the world. The oligarchs can never be trusted. They lie and use "position" to control the Deep State. They spin their stories so they can profit from the public's misconceptions.

The bottom line is: *"There will be no democracy until the public understands the oligarchs and they understand the public will not condone collusion."*

The solutions are staring the public in the face. First, the masses need to take care of the elderly. Give an older person the equivalent of a basic military person's pension. Make sure he has a good medical program. That money should flow back into the economy.

Next, install a tax system to bring financial inequalities in line. The wealthy brought us this dead-end. They took advantage of a crooked system. Trickle-down was nonsense. Ignore what Bill Gates, Mark Cuban, Ray Dalio, Tudor Jones, George Soros, and the other billionaires say. Do the opposite! Tax the wealthy as hard or harder than they were taxed after WW II.

I was pleased to see a French economist, Gabriel Zucman, publish *The Triumph of Injustice: How the Rich Dodge Taxes and How to Make Them Pay*. Zucman provides the math and theory of why a tax of the rich will work.

Next, pay the unemployed a livable wage because there will be far fewer jobs in the near future. As long as the military is funded in a biased manner, the non-elite part of society needs a safety net. At the same time, focus on reducing our military. Our government and the other powers need to solve this issue so we can pursue real issues. We need to join other super-powers and solve the population problem so we are not pressed to make quick decisions. We need to stop ruining our planet.

Putting the safety net up and getting back to a sound financial system is stage one. Stage two could run concurrently and it should give the public control.

The public should reduce the role of the CIA and set up a Department of National Public Intelligence [DNPI]. The DNPI director should be elected. The DNPI should track the elites - every word and ownership record would be recorded. There's ample storage capacity on the government's cloud system. The public will need video, and every citizen should have access to the data.

The DNPT would set up a complete accounting of money, stocks, and property. There should be no unknown ownerships. All property should be unique and traceable - no un-numbered accounts. The proper appraisal values would be applied to assets and the public should be able to view all the records of all the people.

Our fiat money could be replaced with a cryptocurrency. Any money off the books should be rendered worthless. This type of control should help eliminate drug trafficking and money laundering, and that could shut down the mafias.

The public needs to know who the rich are. Anyone with a billion dollars needs to be under a spyglass. Ditto for the President, the Deep State, CEO of large corporations, etc.

The DNPI should administer lie detector and drug tests regularly to all the oligarchs and their Deep State until they are retrained. That should put everything in place, back to where it was. Why not? They are the problem.

New laws and systems should empower individuals. We need free Internet and cell phones. Corporations and advertisers might have to be excluded from that space. Control of the media and the Internet needs to be put in the hands of the public.

The publishing business structure should be rebuilt away from Jewish influence. Only then will the media present true public opinion.

Trump was as Rex Tillerson defined him - devoid of professionalism. Forget Trump! In the grand scheme of things, the president is a puppet, albeit he can be dangerous without a Mattis and Barr to contain him.

The Catholics and the Israelis are the team. Everything starts with the oligarchs and pawns like William Barr. Barr saved Trump on the impeachment. Barr met with Murdock in New York to discuss the Catholic-Judean relationship after Trump and FOX got into a flap.

Barr was most important because a rigid rule of law is the oligarchs' primary tool for retaining control. Oligarchs use a set of static laws to retain their money and power. The laws are written for the oligarchs!

Trump's last SCOTUS nominee was Amy Coney Barrett, a graduate of Notre Dame. A prior Trump appointee, Brett Kavanaugh, was Catholic. Trump positioned the rich Roman Catholics and the Jews for at least a generation.

The Catholics are on board with the other elite groups even though Jack Kennedy was assassinated. The Catholics and the Jewish Syndicate are a powerful alliance. One can't expect these groups to pivot and support changes to the Grand Area plans. It has served their purpose to rule the world.

The Catholics are the king of the hill. The Catholics got their SCOTUS appointments and the Pope brushed off Pompeo's request for an audience.

China inked a deal with the Catholics because the Catholics have the money and the people power. I believe Barr, Trump, and Biden were Catholic. Just add it all up!

The intelligence community with its databases could help to define a brighter future. The new generation of computer-savvy intellectuals could encourage changes. The public needs a few Perot eagles to step outside the box and replace failure with vision and self-reliance. Intellectuals need to make reorganizing an unfair system a legitimate project.

We need to change the world's emphasis to solid, long-term objectives. That is relatively easy to shift in one year if you have control.

As an example, I played in a low-ante Texas Hold'em game with three old friends. I dealt myself an off-suited A-4. Everyone called the ante, and the flop was A-J-4, giving me two pair, aces and fours.

Two pair in Hold'em with just four players should be a winning hand. Seat 1 checks. Seat 2 makes a small bet, and seat 3 raises. Seat 3 is a sharp guy who has just retired and is still learning to play. He is normally a timid bettor. For him to raise, he must have a pretty good hand, probably better than a pair, maybe two pair or three of a kind.

Since he would not have called to begin with on a J-4 and he would raise pre-flop with a pair of jacks or aces, that implies he has three fours, aces and jacks, or aces and fours. Since I have a four, it is more likely he has an ace-jack. Therefore, he has me beat. The only card I can hit to win would be a four, so I fold.

A jack comes on the river and the weak player makes a boat and wins an enormous pot. I breathe a sigh of relief. I avoided losing. In a sense, I have won. Avoiding taking a big loss is like winning. It is so important to look just a little ahead. Experience allowed me to avoid giving my money to this soft player.

If you can avoid the small mistakes and build a safe, secure life without getting in a rush, that's more important than making the big score. I'm old and now I try not to do anything that jeopardizes my assets unless I thoroughly review the situation. If possible, I ask for the advice of others.

I am an expert on this subject because I have made every dumb mistake in the book. I never cared about risk or conservatism – make it, spend it, roll-on, there will always be more. I understood accounting and math, and I had skills and always job opportunities. Since I was semi-conservative, I avoided drugs, so that wasn't a problem.

Life is so much easier if you avoid even smaller mistakes. Start with having the right spouse and not living on the edge. Get a reasonably good job that won't disappear in six months.

When you get older there are no rewards in rehashing the past. The way I operate today is different than what I would have done earlier in life. Now, I look more for longer-term opportunities and friendships. It's important to have a longer-term perspective.

There is a problem today in our society that polarization has caused. There is a macho attitude of aggression against less aggressive neighbors. This is something which is new and counter-productive.

As an example, a friend told me his boy decided to get a Covid test before he came home for the holidays, just to make sure he wasn't bringing the virus home with him. Other students had told him he could charge it to his health insurance, so he did. He didn't even ask what the charges would be, but a few weeks later he received a bill for $1,400 for the remainder of the bill. The medical facility had billed the huge healthcare provider for $2,000 and the insurance paid $600.

If this student had paid cash, the total charge would have been $260. The care center overbilled to see how much they could gouge the insurance company.

I posted a question about how this should be handled. I did get two accurate responses. A lawyer I knew suggested the student take this to the Texas Department of Insurance because they handle this type of problem. Another suggested I go to the Attorney General. What was perplexing was that most responses suggested to ignore the gouging and move on. One even said he charged his test to his insurance and they paid $4,600.

This would not have occurred sixty years ago. People read newspapers and editors wrote meaningful editorials. You also had sales clerks trying to be nice to people. Today everything is too much of a hassle. If you say something, you are more likely to get some smart comment thrown back at you. Americans are not working as a team.

I agreed when Nouriel Roubini said the blockchain was overhyped and that no one would use it. Recently, Roubini said the bitcoin was totally manipulated and would crash. I agree with him again, but the problems I see is that the government seems to be encouraging scams and the greedy may delay reality. That may be why Ray Dalio, the biggest hedge fund operator in the U.S. came out in support of the bitcoin. He probably has a related investment.

When Gerald Kushner can set up a corporation to strip off $617M, three-fifth of a billion dollars in campaign donations and get away with it, we no longer have a government. This is not a nation of public laws. This is a nation of oligarch laws handled by crooked lawyers. But, if you were a Trump supporter, Kushner's action probably was just fine.

A lady said, "It seems like we have less ability to forecast events today. Do you believe that is because of Trump?"

No! We have slid downhill for the last 20 years. Computer databases are taking over and opportunities are disappearing. We moved to big cities and stopped going to family reunions because they were too boring. Many of those solid companies that had good jobs and retirement programs are gone.

Now the wave may be about to reverse, but the thinkers have lost their voice to the clans that control the media.

I know! Wishful thinking, but look in the mirror. We've allowed this situation and we can improve it, if we have the courage to gain a voice.

Rule 27: We have to relearn to survive. We need to go back to the basics and think long-term. Begin to believe we can help to correct this "noise". Begin to believe that truth will sweep aside the oligarchs, but don't get caught in too much drama.

Vote the incumbents out.

Take the optimistic road. Consider the CIA a mafia that needs containment and at the same time can evolve into an honorable group.

Conclusions

It's mostly about money! Several decisions destroyed our financial systems.

First, Woodrow Wilson handed the banking system to individuals and that was equivalent to handing the United States to a small group of oligarchs. Some of the FED investors were Morgans or Rockefellers. The Pope and Queen may have invested. The Israelis could now be managing our banks.

We don't know who owns the FED. It's a private bank with no transparency. That's a mistake. The FED should be nationalized and made transparent, immediately!

Second, when Reagan reduced the taxes from over 70% to less than 30% for the rich, he destroyed the middle class. Taxes should be moved back to over 70% on the rich, and the oligarch's total assets should also be softly taxed. Ownership from outside the U.S. should be taxed at a higher rate.

Taxes serve as a perfect throttle for wealth distribution. Look at our situation this way. When President Trump gave trillions to the rich and his son-in-law set aside $617M for their families, he didn't consider the interests of average citizens. Average working Americans need not consider the interests of oligarchs other than allowing them to exist as normal citizens.

Third, we made a mistake bringing in non-whites trying to get brains and/or cheap labor. We created a society of unwed mothers on welfare. Our immigration system has ruined society. New York politics are a big cause of this.

We need to stop all immigration until we decide on a better solution. We need to employ great analysts to examine our social situations and offer better options. Don't hire lawyers and professors for answers. This is not complex. Our social structures and the Deep State created our problems and they are easily solved, if our nation wishes to solve them.

Fourth, we have lost control of the military. The military has to be meaner than the opposition. LeMay was correct. No one wins a war being a nice guy.

We have been in wars for 75 years because our objective has been to control the world, and now the CIA is running the country for the Catholics and the Jewish Syndicate. There is no room for legitimate capitalism unless one wants to set up a hamburger joint.

What do we do with those thousands of agents in the CIA, FBI, and other agencies that only understand handling drugs, or money, or killing people? Can we integrate them into society? Yes, of course, and the world militaries need to accomplish world peace. That is their problem! They should reduce salaries, retirement benefits, hiring, and other budgets.

When the military reduces their ranks, they should also work with China and Russia to decide on how to reduce the world's population in a fair manner.

Napoleon had this type of problem at one point. He solved it for France.

What do we do with a Pompeo type when he is no longer needed? I guess you let him run for president - right? Plan B is, because of his association with Trump, he loses and does something else.

Fifth, the public has no big picture or they are afraid. Even though this book offers encouragement to improve society, the real world is the country's masses got behind the rule of the oligarchs. Our social issues have gotten too complex to fix piecemeal, and the oligarchs are only concerned with themselves.

The media is the cause of fake news and the public's ignorance. The Academy of Motion Picture Arts and Sciences, the way films are produced and distributed, how television is used as a weapon, the way books and screenplays are controlled, and all aspects of the media need to be rebuilt to release non-fiction truth to bring the public up to date.

Sixth, I think we need a two-term Senate and a three-term House. I think we need at least five different presidents, the four I previously defined and one to define our Grand Area strategy.

It should be obvious; we have a losing strategy. If a society is either too simple, too complex, or pursues the wrong course, it will fail.

The Comanche people had a social structure that was too simple!

"Their government is essentially patriarchal, guided by wise and fraternal councils. They are insensible to the wants and luxuries of civilization, and know neither poverty nor riches, vice or virtue, and are alike exempt from the deplorable vicissitudes of fortune. Theirs is a happy state of social equality, which knows not the perplexities of political ambition or the crimes of avarice."

- Randolph B. Marcy, 1866 [Y50]

The Comanche minimized their perplexities. With their simplistic society, they opted to fight to the last man.

Obviously, the U.S. has pursued a failed course for the last half-century. I didn't mean for this section of the book to sound like a ranting session, but most of the oligarch's pawns are never going to discuss real issues with the public, so nothing will get done. Even worse, the United States has lost its ability to execute efficiently. For example, what happened to the Covid vaccine? A year after Moderna comes up with a solution, an 82-year-old [me] can't go out and get vaccinated? Did Trump sell the vaccine for profit?

There are exceptions. Elizabeth Warren gets it. Consider the cold satire she wrote in her note chief justice John Roberts was forced to read as a question to the Republican impeachment panel: "At a time when the large majorities of Americans have lost faith in government, does the fact that the chief justice is presiding over an impeachment trial in which Republican senators have thus far refused to allow witnesses or evidence contribute to the loss of legitimacy of the chief justice, the Supreme Court and the Constitution."

Mrs. Warren's question was at the heart of our issues. Her problems were her intellectualism and that she was a white female. I am sure she was relieved to see SCOTUS cut Trump off before he could steal the second election.

Thomas Jefferson got it.

"We might as well require a man to wear still the coat which fitted him when a boy, as civilized society to remain under the regimen of their barbarous ancestors. ... Let us follow no such examples, nor weakly believe that one generation is not as capable as another of taking care of itself."

Andrew Yang sees it. Under-privileged workers need a $1,000 a month so they can move to the country, grow a garden, use Zoom, and put trot lines out on Thursday night so they can have fish to eat on Friday.

The public is at huge risk, and few see the black swan. As the world becomes a digital space-world, associate with the right people, and acquire technocrat and leadership skills. Care about others. Pitch in and navigate through the maze. Build a network of family and friends. Take responsibility. Dress sharp; associate with elites and show them you're smart and good for your word. Display patience and focus on raising your children to be problem solvers.

Become an expert at playing position. Recognize that the elites control the social structure and they consider non-elites to be sheep. Embrace entrepreneurship. That may be hard because the world needs less people. Perhaps no one needs to get killed if the public becomes logical and society gains a broader perspective.

This is an opportunity for open-minded people to step back to a more insolated society where people enjoy being with and caring for their neighbors. It's okay to have a beer at the pub every once in a while.

The new digital technology can streamline everything. A person should be able to sit in his cave and see what's happening on the other side of the world in real-time, without traveling.

The doctors and lawyers and executives owning those nice homes need to engage in constructive dialog with the public. The public needs candidates who discuss the potential of the future because the oligarchs' game is not going anywhere.

As just one person in society with no voice, unless you have an extraordinary talent, you can't afford to get in the way of this big slime-ball rolling down the gutter. All you can do is try to understand, discuss real issues, and sleep well because you have carefully attempted to do the honorable things.

Cicero reflected that all he needed was his garden and his library. Today, the library is the Internet, the cell-phone, and a high speed connection.

Let's spend more time watching the little red cork for a strike. There are so many options, and now is the time to think about those alternatives as they apply to the next generation. We don't need to conquer the galaxy before we fix our planet. As my friend John Sandberg would say, "We need to Get-er-done."

After Thoughts

I borrowed heavily from my prior work. Why discard timely material that few people have read? Besides, this dysfunction society will not go away. Don't expect anything from politicians and academia. They are owned by the oligarchs.

This subject needs to be revisited until the sheep fix the system. I want to communicate with others who are non-biased, neither conservative nor liberal - people that enjoy lightly discussing subjects in this book. Send your comments to Burnside24u at Yahoo dot com. If you disagree with everything, that's fine. I didn't write in search of agreement. My thoughts are a question. Thinking and writing are a process.

Harry Markopolos discovered Bernie Madoff's Ponzi scheme. Markopolos tried unsuccessfully for nine years to shut Madoff down. Writers can't walk away from their cause.

I'm sure this book has several mistakes and omissions. Help me correct any problems you see.

References

Anderson, Christopher. *Jack and Jackie*, Avon Books, NY, 1997.

Brands, H.W. *Traitor to His Class*, Doubleday, NY, 2008.

Burnside, Robert Schramm. *Coup d'Etat*, Soleil Press, Lisbon Falls, ME, 2003.

Burnside, Robert Schramm. *JFK and the World Oligarchy*, Soleil Press, Lisbon Falls, ME, 2012.

Burnside, Robert Schramm. *2020 – The Year of the New World Order*, Soleil Press, Lisbon Falls, ME, 2020.

Chomsky, Noam. *Who Rules the World*, Metropolitan Books, New York, NY, 2016.

Dochery, Gerry and Macgregor, Jim. *Hidden History, The Secret Origins of the First World War*, Mainstream Publishing, Edinburgh and London, 2013.

Falk, Richard. *Power Shift on the New Global Order*, Zed Books Ltd, London, 2016.

Fertitta, Tilman. *Shut Up and Listen*, Harper Collins Leadership, 2019.

Feifer, Gregory. *Russians*, Twelve, Hachette Book Group, NY, 2014.

Finnegan, Conor. "President Trump is not "fit for office …", Yahoo, 2020.

Gombrich, E.H. *A Little History of the World*, Yale University Press, New Haven and London, 2008.

Hartman, Kenneth E. "Life after Life", Harper's, October, 2019.

Hedges, Chris. *America: The Farewell Tour*, Simon & Schuster, NY, 2018.

Hersh, Seymour. *The Dark side of Camelot*, Back Bay Books, NY, 1997.

Kasich, John. *Two Paths*, St. Martin's Press, NY, NY, 2017.

Kinzer, Stephen. *The Brothers, John Foster Dulles and Allen Dulles, and Their Secret World War*, Time Books, Henry Holt and Company, LLC, NY. NY, 2013.

Kyncl, Robert, with Peyvan, Maany. *Streampunks*, Virgin Books, London, 2017.

Law, Lisa. *Interviews with Icons*, Lumen Books, 2000.

Levitsky, Steven & Ziblatt, Daniel. How Democracies Die, Penguin Books, NY, 2018.

Mallon, Thomas. "Ambassador in Spite of Himself," The New York Times Book Review, December 31, 2000.

Mayer, Jane. *Dark Money*, Anchor Books, NY, 2016.

Mises, Ludwig von. Mises Institute, Auburn, Alabama. [There are a large number of publications of books and papers by Misses covering post-WW I Germany and the Federal Reserve including *The Case Against the FED*.]

Neeley, Bill. Quanah Parker and His People, Brazos Press, Slaton, TX, 1986.

Nelson, Phillip F. *LBJ: From Mastermind to the "Colossus"*, Skyhorse Publishing, NY, NY, 2014.

Newman, Jesse and McGroarty, Patrick. "The Next Farm Bust is Coming," The Wall Street Journal, February 9, 2017.

Powell, J. Alfred. "How FDR Forced Japan to Attack Pearl Harbor While Lying About Trying to Avoid War", LewRockwell.com, July 25, 2019.

Prouty, L. Fletcher, *JFK*, Skyhorse Publishing, NY, NY, 2011.

Quigley, Carroll. *Tragedy & Hope*, Macmillan Company, NY, 1966.

Rockefeller, David. *Memoirs*, Random House, NY, 2002.

Schindler, John R. "The Real Russian Mole Inside NSA," *Observer*, August 23, 2016.

Sebestyen, Victor. *Lenin*, Pantheon Books, NY, 2017.

Summers, Anthony. *Official and Confidential*, G. P. Putman's Sons, New York, 1993.

Tabatabai, Arman. "Study says the U.S. is losing its Entrepreneurial Edge", 2018.

Thomas, Gordon. *Gideon's Spies*, St. Martin's Press, NY, 1999.

Twyman, Noel. *Bloody Treason*, Laurel Publishing, CA, 1997.

Unz, Ron. "American Pravda: Our Deadly World of Post-War Politics", LewRockwell.com, July 23, 2019.

Ward, Vicky. *Kushner, Inc.*, St. Martin's Press, NY, 2019.

Webb, Walter Prescott. *The Great Frontier*, University of Texas Press, Austin, 1952.

Wolff-Mann, Ethan. "The Federal Reserve contributes to Inequality: Former FDIC Chair", Yahoo, June 8. 2020.

Notes

Y01 Hedges: America: The Farewell Tour 138

Y02 Mallon: Ambassador in Spite of Himself

Y03 Hartman: "Life after Life", 65

Y04 Fertitta: Shut Up and Listen, 197

Y05 Anderson: Jack and Jackie, 175

Y06 Burnside: Coup d'Etat, 41

Y07 Mayer: Dark Money, 65

Y08 Finnegan: "President Trump is not fit for office …"

Y09 Brands: Traitor to His Class, 824

Y10 Prouty: JFK, xxiii

Y11 Dochery: Hidden History, 14 and other pages

Y12 Quigley: Tragedy & Hope, 131-133

Y13 Kinzer: The Brothers, 323

Y14 Levitsky: How Democracies Die, 170-171

Y15 Sebestyen: Lenin, 374

Y16 Dochery: Hidden History, 333 and other pages

Y17 Nelson: JFK, From Mastermind to "The Colossus", 198

Y18 Mises: Mises Institute publications

Y19 Prouty: JFK, xxviii

Y20 Chomsky: Who Rules the World, 45

Y21 Prouty: JFK, 12

Y22 Summers: Official and Confidential, 259

Y23 Prouty: JFK, xxviii

Y24 Prouty: JFK, 17-18

Y25 Prouty: JFK, 41

Y26 Rockefeller: Memoirs, 406

Y27 Kasich: Two Paths, 4

Y28 Hersh: The Dark Side of Camelot, 135

Y29 Hersh: The Dark Side of Camelot, 152

Y30 Rockefeller: Memoirs, 149

Y31 Thomas: Gideon's Spies, 54, 96

Y32 Mises: The Case Against the FED, 133

Y33 Wolff-Mann: "The Federal Reserve contributes to Inequality"

Y34 Unz: "American Pravda: Our Deadly World of Post-War Politics"

Y35 Burnside: JFK and the World Oligarchy, 94

Y36 Kyncl: Streampunks, 156

Y37 Tabatabai: "Study says U.S. is losing its Entrepreneurial Edge".

Y38 Falk: Power Shift on the New Global Order, 189

Y39 Schindler: "The Real Russian Mole Inside NSA"

Y40 Schindler: "The Real Russian Mole Inside NSA"

Y41 Twyman: Bloody Treason, 667

Y42 Twyman: Bloody Treason, 671

Y43 Neeley: Quanah Parker and His People, 171

Y44 Quigley: Tragedy & Hope, 1247

Y45 Feifer: Russians, 327

Y46 Law: Interviews with Icons, 108-111

Y47 Gombrich: A Little History of the World, 205

Y48 Levitsky: How Democracies Die 170-171

Y49 Falk: Power Shift on the New Global Order, 223

Y50 Neeley: Quanah Parker and His People, 131